SEVERED DREAMS
RECONSTRUCTING YOUR PURPOSE

Chad Porter   Mike Voorheis

ISBN 978-10987503-0-5

Foreword

Chad Porter is one of the most genuine people I have had the pleasure to know. The Ziglar team was honored to have Chad become Ziglar Legacy Certified to represent us through his work.

All of us—Chad's Ziglar Legacy Certification class included—were deeply and sincerely impressed by him and his story. Time did not allow us to learn many of the details of Chad's accident and ensuing struggles and victories, so reading his book has been enlightening—and very encouraging—to me. It only allows me to admire him more.

Character is the missing ingredient in so much of our country's and our world's societies today. Chad Porter's story portrays a character rarely evidenced but increasingly necessary if we hope to continue to enjoy our God-given freedoms and responsibilities. I believe *Chad Porter, Severed Dreams* is foundational to re-igniting the spark of character that will help us to rebuild and strengthen our own lives, as well as help to structure the lives of our children and grandchildren. It is my hope and prayer that this book will find its way into the hands of those who are not only equipped but willing to put it to use in their homes, businesses, and communities.

Sincerely,
Tom Ziglar, CEO
Ziglar, Inc.

Prologue

Have you ever experienced a moment in time where everything in your life is right on track and you are destined to achieve the big plans you have set for your future? As a young teenager, I was in that enviable position—everything seemed to be going just the way I wanted. I was a good student, class president, and one of the best athletes in my class at Lumberton Junior High. Each day, a feeling of excitement, freedom, and optimism radiated from me with the confidence that no obstacles could keep me from achieving my dreams. Somebody my age was eventually going to be a professional athlete, so why shouldn't that be me?

As adults, we don't often muster that level of excitement about what the future holds. We don't truly enjoy the peaks of life, because we have toiled so long in the valleys. If you're not focused on your purpose, you can come to subsist in a safe, stable plain where success and unabashed joy exist only on a distant horizon.

If you think back to your teenage years, you were full of promise. No matter your circumstances, it was a time where you began to mold yourself and figure out who you wanted to be. You still had control of your future—what field you would pursue, where you would live, who you would marry, and how you would make your mark on the world.

As adults, we live with our choices. Do we live up to our potential? Are we successful in the matters that are most important to us? Adulthood makes us more rigid, and the consequences are more severe if we decide to change our path. If you minimize your risk, you can continue to live in your comfort zone, but you will never achieve anything spectacular. It's never too late to change your path. As long as you have a breath, you have a chance.

During my early teens, I felt invincible. I was chasing my dreams and capitalizing on my opportunities. Nobody had given me a good reason why I couldn't be an NFL star, and I built my future around becoming a professional football player. It was gonna happen! I had the skills, body, work ethic, intelligence, and drive. I was indestructible and oblivious. Nothing could ruin my plans!

Chapter 1:
Skis to Success

White Lake

During the school year, I was a star of the football and basketball teams, winner of a few Best All-Around awards and playing a main role in both church and school theatrical productions.

During the summer, I was a proud member of the Ski Heels, a semi-professional water ski troupe. Among the summer campers at White Lake, North Carolina, the Ski Heels were royalty.

I had been chasing the back end of a boat since I was 4 years old. It's what you do when you live on the lake for the summer.

Both of my parents worked in education and they were devoted to giving my sister and me an unforgettable childhood, anchored in spirituality and structure and splashed with adventure and excitement.

To say we were blessed as kids would be an understatement. Our parents provided what we needed, not always what we wanted. So, we learned the value of hard work at a young age.

Every summer, we packed up our house and headed to our little spot in paradise. White Lake might not be what most people consider paradise, but for a kid from rural Lumberton, North Carolina, it was everything.

I learned to ski before I learned to tie my shoes. I loved the exhilaration of cruising across the water behind a powerful boat. And when your mom is worried about your safety, but your dad says, "He can do it," you feel like the bravest 4-year-old in the world. Budding athletes learn to imitate the swing of their favorite home run hitter or the jump shot of their favorite basketball player. As a budding skier, we needed only to look out on the lake to be inspired by our local legends of the water, the White Lake Ski Heels.

From the early 1970s to the early 1990s, the Ski Heels performed stunts that you might see in a movie like *Jaws 3*. Though the Ski Heels were just teenagers who sometimes performed for only dozens of spectators, their skill on the water rivaled that of the performers at Cypress Gardens, the Florida theme park that draws thousands of paying customers every weekend.

For years, I spent my summers watching the teenagers and trying to imitate their tricks. By the time my voice dropped, I had excelled to the point where I earned an offer to ski with the Ski Heels! For the next few years, I learned the ropes . . . and the flips and the tricks. I was loving every moment of it.

We didn't have professional trainers, expert coaches or an unlimited budget to buy the latest ski gear. But we did have supportive parents, unbridled teenage energy, reckless spirits and just enough maturity to understand the line between taking a risk and being completely idiotic. Mostly.

We did all our training at White Lake, where you could hook up your RV, enjoy a stunning view of the sunset over the water, and step back in time about 30 years.

During June and July, our practice sessions started as soon as we rolled out of the beds in our trailers and campers and lasted until the red light on the White Lake water tower signaled us to head back in. Most days, my parents would catch a glimpse of me passing by in the boat or maybe at lunchtime, if I brought some friends over; otherwise, I was on the water till dark.

White Lake is a quaint resort with crystal clear water and white sand. It was a kid's paradise and was marketed as the "Nation's Safest Beach," perhaps because there has never been a rip current, a shark bite, or even a jellyfish sting at the freshwater lake. Many small inns and cottages offered rooms at reasonable prices, but most visitors stayed in trailers or campers, the working-class man's "place at the beach." There was no pretension, no posturing, and the biggest splash was made not by the biggest yacht, but by our shoestring-budget ski team. Visitors to White Lake mostly came from four counties surrounding Bladen County, and we all shared the same upbringing, the same drawl and the same appreciation for blue-collar fun.

Goldston's Beach was the hub of White Lake, featuring an arcade, a mini-amusement park, the most competitive of Bingo parlors, putt-putt golf, waterslides and a place to sit in the shade with a burger and a Dairy Queen Blizzard on a scorching July afternoon.

Distractions were plentiful for teenage boys, and water skiing was a good way to start a conversation with a cute girl who would be on the lake for a week. A good opening line could set the stage for the ultra-romantic late-night cruise. With an acoustic guitar and the inspiration of Boyz 2 Men, teenage boys would serenade pretty girls. The singing may not have been worthy of a *Star Search* appearance, but our local status, and the fact we had a boat, made up for any lacking vocal talent. Even a long day in late June seemed too short to capture all the energy and vitality of the scene. Each night was filled with anticipation of what the next day might bring. Life was simple, and while we milked it for every ounce of exhilaration, we never stopped to appreciate it.

During the daily practice sessions, we experimented with what we could push our bodies to do. We really should have had EMS standing by on the beach, because every maneuver was a potential medical emergency. A barefoot skier could catch a pinky toe in the water—a miniscule mistake that would send him flipping and skipping uncontrollably across the water, which was as unforgiving as parking lot cement when you skidded across it at 35 miles per hour. Violent body slams into the water literally turned our eyelids inside out, bloodied our noses, and knocked the wind out of us. And water rushed into every opening—yes, like a freshwater enema—of our bodies.

We could have filled up a complete season of *America's Funniest Home Videos* as our bodies recklessly tumbled, bounced and skidded across White Lake.

One oversight could put a skier in a precarious position. Like the time we forgot to wet the jump ramp properly as one of our buddies was laying down a sharp cut to hit the ramp at the perfect speed. Unfortunately, the friction of the dry ramp stopped his skis dead cold as soon as they hit the ramp, sending the teen slamming face first into the ramp. His limp body bounced and skidded up the ramp with just enough momentum to fall over the peak into the lake. Coincidentally, he landed right next to the two guys were who were supposed to be wetting the ramp. I don't think the full body bruises were soothed by the culprits when the only thing they had to say was, "Oops, we didn't realize you were that close."

As long as nobody needed medical attention, we enjoyed the laughs on the boat, and we'd relive every detail during lively conversations later, using our battle scars as visual cues to retell the story to anyone who would listen.

The grueling practices, however, provided more than just great laughs to share. We learned lessons—we never had another dry jump ramp—that prepared us for moments like the Tucker Lake show, when we could make a small-town crowd *ooh and aah* at maneuvers they couldn't see anywhere else without traveling hundreds of miles.

Tucker Lake

Nestled on the corner of interstates 40 and 95, you will find Tucker Lake. Owned by the Tucker Family, it's a 30-acre utopia where locals can cool off and enjoy a family day beating the blistering Carolina heat.

The Tuckers wanted to do something extra special for their community, so they hired the Ski Heels to bring our four powerful ski boats and entire ski team to put on a show that their patrons would never forget.

I was so pumped for our first show of the year that I was oblivious to the coffee table in the middle of our lake house. As I ran through the house that morning, I kicked it really hard with a shoeless foot. The pinky toenail on that left foot was no competition for that hard-oak leg. It peeled that little nail all the way back, so it was barely holding on by a thread of skin—flapping in the wind, bleeding profusely! I don't know if you have ever felt a heartbeat in your toe before, but I felt like Daffy Duck after an anvil dropped on his foot. Pulsing!

Pain surrendered to panic when I realized that I was a couple hours away from my first ski show of the season, and I had a toenail blowing in the breeze. The thought of sliding that foot into tight rubber ski boots was horrifying! I called a friend on the team to explain how I wasn't going to be able to go to the show. I was looking for comfort and understanding, but my friend merely ridiculed me and questioned my manhood until I agreed that a pinky toe injury wouldn't keep me off the water.

I turned to my dad, the consummate problem solver. He was more than happy to help me find a way to deal with the dangling toenail. I should have been a little skeptical with his enthusiasm, but I trusted his judgement. The next thing I know he's handing me a pair of pliers.

"Just grab that nail as tight as you can and snatch it off," he said. "It will be like pulling off a Band-Aid."

Ummm, no! It will not feel like pulling off a Band-Aid! But I'm tough, I'm an athlete, I can handle it.

I squeezed that pitiful nail tight, braced for the pain, counted to three and . . . I released the pliers before the pull.

I couldn't go through with it. My dad understood my commitment issues in holding the tool long enough to finish the job, so he found me a pair of vise-grip pliers. "Problem solved" he said. "Just lock down on that nail and throw them across the room. It will be like pulling out a loose tooth." I swear to you, if cell phones had existed, he would have been videoing the whole ordeal to put it on YouTube. I still couldn't do it. I was beginning to question my own manhood.

So, I went underneath the sink and found the perfect solution, redneck chrome! Yes, redneck chrome—also known as duct tape. If MacGyver can build an airplane out of duct tape, it must be strong enough to hold on a pinky toenail.

I pushed the nail down as far as I could and wrapped it as tight as I could stomach. The bleeding stopped, and it wasn't flapping loosely anymore. I was ready for the show and excited to spend an epic day with my buddies doing what we do best—showing off on the water.

When the ski team hit the water at Tucker Lake, mothers put down the sunscreen, kids stopped splashing, fathers lifted babies on their shoulders. In a time before wakeboards gained popularity, our skiers' athletic barrel rolls and complete flips were the pinnacle of athleticism on the water.

At the beginning of the show, our barefoot skiers captured the attention of the families on the beach. One skier dropped into the water from a height of 12 feet, popped up behind the power boat and skied barefoot around the lake before dismounting with a dramatic head-first flip.

We had some supremely gifted kids on our team, Danny Faircloth being one of the more talented of the bunch. He could do a trick that seemed to defy logic—a 360-degree circle around the boat. He would ski wide over the wake and gain so much momentum that he could slingshot himself around the front of the boat that was pulling him as the driver turned the vessel sharply in the opposite direction going under Danny's ski rope. It would take a physics professor to explain it, but even a grade-schooler could appreciate it.

One of my acts was less about awe-inspiring athleticism and more about shriek-inducing entertainment. In between acts, I pulled on a hot, heavy gorilla suit and snuck down to the beach. There I found one mother so engaged with her children that she didn't notice the approaching gorilla. I sat down close enough where she could sense my presence. Her kids' mouths gaped open, and when she finally looked over her shoulder, she was startled by her first glimpse of the furry black creature on her blanket. She screamed and pushed me away playfully, and I chased the kids across the sand. They screamed with delight until the heat inside the suit overwhelmed me, and I had to dash back out to the dock to take off the mask and catch my breath.

The episode on the beach foreshadowed one of my favorite acts. A gorilla on the beach is a sight some of those kids will never forget. But who has ever seen a gorilla on water skis?

The crowd loved the spectacle, but it wasn't easy to orchestrate. As soon as the gorilla suit hit the lake, it absorbed so much water that the depth of the lake dropped about six inches. And in that waterlogged, hundred-pound gorilla costume, I skied across the lake, chasing Martha Huggins, a year older than me and one of the coolest chicks in all of Southeastern North Carolina.

My boat chased hers, swinging me wide enough to get within arm's reach, before she slipped away in the opposite direction. Finally, I got enough momentum, dropped my rope and slid across the water, where I grabbed her around the waist, my skis outside of hers. For once, the crowd was on the beast's side, applauding when I reached the beauty. Martha shimmied away and, using a ski rope she had discreetly passed to me, I chased her across the wake behind her boat until she finally submitted to my charms. Together, we skied one last lap around the lake for our adoring spectators. It was Americana at its finest—small-town crowds being entertained by talented kids whose only real reward was a smile on a child's face and scattered applause from the lake shore.

After the gorilla act, all that remained of our show was the pyramid, an act that we had practiced by tying our ropes to a cypress tree on the shore back at our home base, White Lake. During practices, the bottom row would assume skiers' stances and teach the lightweights where to step and where not to step as they ascended. On the ground beneath cypress tree, a fall could lead to a dogpile of laughter. But at 25 mph on the water, the danger was very real. A backward fall could be painful. A forward fall could mean getting run over by at least one pair of skis. And if a base lost his balance, the collapsing pyramid would surely mean some serious bruises and scrapes—if we were lucky.

The rope lengths had to be precise and specific to each skier, and our organizers—volunteer parents—made sure they were measured to the inch.

We had accomplished what we traveled two hours to do—give a crowd of locals an experience they wouldn't soon forget. After the ramp jumpers, the comedy acts, the trick skiers, and the wild and crazy bare footers, we prepared for the Grand Finale.

The pyramid was daunting, but we'd rehearsed it so often that we might have been able to do it blindfolded. Fortunately, we never tried it that way. The question on this Saturday at Tucker Lake was, "Would we even have time to build the pyramid?"

Dark clouds stacked on the horizon across Interstate 40 as the nine of us perched on the floating dock. An imminent Carolina summer thunderstorm was building rapidly. It could swallow itself up and disappear, or it could erupt into a terrifying barrage of stinging rain, lightning and ground-shaking thunder.

The Ski Heels parents kept a wary eye on the foreboding sky, long before apps could tell you that the nearest streak of lightning was 3.61 miles away. Their other eye was on us, and they could see how badly we wanted to build the pyramid. They made a calculated decision that the storm was far enough away and that we could complete our final act.

The ski boat—powerful enough to pull nine skiers at 20-25 mph—thundered from the dock. The four kids on the top row didn't need skis; they sat on our laps on the floating dock with their feet on top of our ski boots and we'd wrap our arms around them to keep them with us as the boat pulled us up. When the boat took off, the bases stood strong, and the younger boys and the sisters started climbing. Foot on thigh, hand on head, next foot on shoulder blade. Within seconds, they were all up, arms locked at the shoulders as the girls waved to the crowd with their outside arms, covered by long-sleeved, sparkly red swimsuits. After circling the lake a couple times to the delight of the crowd, the upper tier climbed down, and we all released our ski ropes in perfect synchronization.

Then we climbed into the boat for an easy ride back to the dock. Our stunt had been successful, and another day of risk-taking on the water was coming to an end. For a few brief moments, the looming clouds were forgotten amid the euphoria of accomplishment and pleasure of entertaining a crowd of strangers.

It was time to pack up, and we all had jobs to do.

Each team member had a role in the show and also in packing up. If one person didn't carry their weight, somebody else had to pick it up for them. We certainly had our fair share of fun traveling with the Ski Heels, but we learned so much more, with teamwork and dependability at the top of the list.

Two fathers guided the boat back up to the floating dock that traveled with our team. At about 20 yards short of the shore, they turned the rear of the boat toward dry land to give us all plenty of room to exit and start the loading up process. All nine skiers, still in a celebratory mood, scrambled toward shore behind the idling boat in waist-deep water, helping to meticulously organize the ropes and skis. Packing was as orchestrated as the performance. The storm was looming, the wind was picking up, and we needed to get off the water.

As it turns out, lightning wasn't what we needed to be worried about.

Chapter 2:
Blood in the Water

Defining Moment

I was directly behind the boat, flanked by other Ski Heels, when I was startled by the unmistakable sound of an engine gunning full throttle. Frightened screams surrounded me. As two dads were emptying the boat of skis and ropes the unthinkable, improbable happened.

The ski boat, with its 400-horsepower engine, had accidentally slipped into reverse and was charging at my teammates and me at full speed. Michael Pittman, one of my best friends, leapt to the side with my other teammates, but I was directly in line. I never even had the chance to look back to see what was happening. In that one fraction of a second, I decided to dive headfirst away from the boat and go as deep as I could swim. Instinctively, I thought that if I dove all the way to the sand, that I could slip under the boat and avoid any danger.

That decision may have very well saved my life that day. One thing is for sure, it certainly changed it.

That one moment has led me to feel helpless and hopeful. It has helped me experience humility and some of the most gratifying experiences that life can offer. It has shaped me into the man I am today.

I dove away from the charging boat, but even through the muffling water, I could hear the eerie, high-pitched hissing of the propeller screaming louder and louder as it tracked toward me.

My head and torso were out of harm's way, but within a second and a half, my legs were sucked into the steel propeller, a giant blender blade rotating at about 4,000 revolutions per minute. My legs thrashed around limply as the propeller pulverized them, slashing and crushing them and slinging my body around like a rag doll.

Terror gripped me, but adrenaline stopped the pain signals before they could reach my brain. I could feel my legs being pummeled repeatedly by the blades, which flipped me onto my back. My chest and face slid across the cool, slick bottom of the boat as my hands searched for a grip.

After only a few prolonged seconds of chaos, I felt a jolt. The boat had hit a docked boat, and the driver scrambled to his feet and shut off the engine, stopping the propellers and releasing the suction on my legs.

Finally, I could reach the metal support bar for the wooden platform at the back of the boat. I knew that I shouldn't try to put my feet to the ground or crawl out from underneath the boat because my legs were severely injured. I floated myself backward and my face crested.

The remaining spectators and the Ski Heels couldn't tell that my legs had been mangled under the boat. All they knew was that I had been behind the boat when it bolted into gear and I hadn't surfaced.

When I pulled my head and shoulders out from under the boat, Michael had the goofiest smile in pure relief.

He was thinking "Wow, this is great. Chad survived, and he's perfectly fine. He's not even hurt."

But he was so, so wrong.

I told him, "Michael, it got my legs."

"It's OK," he said, trying to convince us both. "Everything's gonna be all right."

But he couldn't have imagined the carnage that had occurred under the boat.

Michael grabbed me with one arm under the backs of my knees and the other under the back of my neck, cradling me as he started to lift me out of the water.

When he lifted me, he could see two inches of bone jutting out of the right leg. Blood sprayed two feet up in the air. The pool of blood-red water expanded around me.

I could see only the right leg, and I was horrified. It looked as if someone had planted a stick of dynamite inside my lower leg and it had exploded. All I saw for those brief seconds that I could stomach looking was shredded meat and exposed broken bones. The whiteness of several inches of exposed shin bone etched a shuddering image that has never been erased. Even as I returned my eyes to the sky, I could still see the fountain of blood that would squirt into the air with each beat of my heart.

Like me, Michael still remembers every vivid detail—the smell of the blood mixed with boat fumes, the distinct feel of the wind— just as clearly as he did 28 years ago. To this day, when he hears the pitch of a screaming engine at a very specific pitch, Michael cringes.

The vision of my mangled legs extinguished the hopeful smile on Michael's face. Covered in my blood, without a word, he lowered me back into the water.

It was a slow-motion moment, one where the gravity of the situation was conveyed through the locked eyes of teenage boys who hadn't conjured a thought not related to girls or sports since fourth grade.

As boys in search of adventure, there were always near-misses to laugh about once the shock and danger had subsided. But this time was different. I had not narrowly escaped a bottle rocket zooming toward my eye. I had not veered my bicycle out of the way of the car seconds before impact. No, this had really happened.

Despite the bloodshed he had seen, Michael kept his head. He wanted to keep the spectators and my teammates from being exposed to the gory sight of a leg that looked like it had been obliterated by a bomb. He pulled me to the floating dock, finally lifting me out of the water. Some people ran toward us to help; others saw the carnage, stopped and backed away.

I don't think Michael Pittman could tell you how he kept his composure. He was an 18-year-old kid confronted with a gruesome, traumatic reality. One of his friends had been severely injured and was lying in his arms. Even as his brain was struggling to grasp the severity of what I was facing, he found the courage to help.

You don't get to choose when you will be tested. But every minute of your life, you're preparing for it. You learn to take responsibility. You learn to accept negative outcomes. You build character by helping others. And when tragedy strikes, you might be prepared to act whether you know it or not.

It's amazing how God grants us the courage to do incredible things that seem unimaginable at the time. In those moments you have to trust that you can make a difference, and hesitation isn't an option.

Up to the point when Michael lifted me up onto the dock, I hadn't felt a lot of pain. I had felt the gnashing pressure of the blades, and I had felt the clutches of the propeller as it held me and punished me with each revolution.

But as the adults came over to try to stop the bleeding and keep me alive until an ambulance arrived, my pain was no longer muted by adrenaline or nervous shock. I could feel every crunch of the broken bones twisting and rubbing against each other and excruciating pressure as blood was quickly draining from my body.

As I lay on the dock in the middle of this chaotic scene, I looked anywhere but down. My right thumb had been split in two when I extricated myself and the tendon had shot back up into my hand. On any other day, this would have been a devastating injury, but on this day, it seemed like a mere scratch.

My best friends, the teenagers I'd laughed and joked with from breakfast till the lights on the lake sent us home every day of the summer, dropped to their hands and knees. Screaming, crying, praying, hugging—they were overwhelmed by fits of anger, confusion and despair.

My life forever changed that day, and so did theirs. The traumatic, gruesome sight is branded into their memories forever. It was as if they had been exposed to a battlefield injury without a second to prepare.

There's a little part of me that is glad that I was underneath the boat instead of witnessing such a horrific act that can never be erased from memory. I can't imagine what it was like to watch that all go down and feel so helpless.

Road to Despair

I frantically looked for two people that I needed desperately. My parents had never missed anything I had ever participated in. If they weren't coaching, they were cheering and distributing snacks to the team. They were always there. In the chaos of the moment, I realized that this was the first ski show my parents had ever missed.

A friend's parent had telephoned my mother and father. This was 1991, so there were no cell phones, no instant messages—delivering the message that no parent ever wants to receive. He told my parents that I had been in an accident and that they should get in the car immediately and meet them at the local hospital.

But my father, understandably, demanded more information. His son was being rushed to the hospital and he needed to know why—NOW!

I cannot fathom how my parents felt when they learned that I had been run over by a boat and that friends and strangers were desperately fighting to save my life on a makeshift dock.

The unknown . . . The helpless feeling . . . The guilt of not being there . . . An emotional rollercoaster . . .

Mom was still recovering from surgery, but she jumped in the Jeep with Dad, who raced NASCAR-style up 68 miles of two-lane roads from White Lake to Smithfield, barely slowing down for the occasional curve or a slower driver in their lane.

Remember, there were no cell phones, no text updates on my condition, just the two of them in the Jeep with a vision in their minds of what might await at the hospital.

Seeing the streaking Jeep Cherokee barreling down the highway into town, a state trooper blue-lighted them. Dad pulled over but immediately told the trooper, "OK, write me a ticket, but I've got to get to the hospital. My son was in an accident, and we have to go!" The trooper, understanding the urgency, sent them right on their way wishing them good luck and to be safe.

As I lay on the wooden dock, which was nearly submerged by all of those who were trying to find some way to help, I had some time to think.

To that point in my life, I had always been in control of my own destiny. Gently steered in the right direction by my parents, I had never felt there was anything I couldn't achieve. This feeling of invincibility was a great motivator. If I did the things I was supposed to do and worked hard, my future was limitless. This included my aspirations in sports. If I wanted to play college football, even pro football, I was limited only by how hard I worked and the choices I made.

So, I had to reconcile this situation with my damaged legs. I knew I had suffered severe injuries to both of my legs. I wasn't thinking that the massive blood loss was a threat to my life; I was devising a plan to be back on the football field in August.

I had broken an arm twice, and from my experience I learned that you can heal and eventually regain all of your strength and mobility. Why should this be anything different? *The doctors can put the bones back together and sew up all the meat and skin and within 8-10 weeks,* I thought, *I ought to be good to go.*

I mentally prepared myself for a wasted summer counting the days until the cast came off, but I convinced myself that I would be back on the football field by August.

This is going to be OK. I have a plan now. I can fix this through the power of positive thinking. Who fought harder than anyone else on the fields and courts to get to his level of athletic prowess? I did. There is nothing that can be thrown at me that I can't handle!

As I was planning my recovery in my head and watching the blood steadily drip from my thumb, I noticed a frantic atmosphere that seemed more urgent than what my current knowledge of the situation warranted.

This will be OK, people. Just stop the bleeding and get me to the hospital to be put back together.

Amid the chaos I heard someone demand a mask and snorkels. "Someone run up to the office and see if they have some. We need them now!"

I was understandably confused. What could they possibly be doing that would require play toys while I was lying on the dock awaiting an ambulance?

That's when I found out just how serious my injuries were. The next words I heard will be as vivid 50 years from now as I heard them that day. "We need to see if we can find his foot!"

What I thought I had control over all came to a crashing halt with one sentence. *You need to find my foot? You must be mistaken. There is no way that I have had a foot cut off and didn't know it. Right?* Remember when Michael lifted me out of the water, and I noticed all the carnage of my right leg? There was a reason I didn't notice the left one—the propeller had made a surgical-like cut in the lower leg and had cut it right off. My size 13 left foot and my hopes of ever playing pro football had sunk into the murky, churned, bloody waters.

My perspective changed immediately from hopeful to desperate.

What did I do to deserve this? Will I ever walk again? Will I ever play sports again? Will I ever be normal again? Is this the end of life as I know it? I had just convinced myself that I could recover from this broken leg—stitch me up, put me in a cast, and I'll be OK.

But when I found out I had lost a foot, naivete had disappeared and there was no hope left to buoy my spirits. I wanted to die. I needed to escape this situation. I begged Michael: "Get a ski, hit me as hard as you can in the head. Please, just knock me out!"

I know you have all experienced an unforgettable nightmare that woke you from a dead sleep, in a cold sweat and clenching a pillow. This dream was not like the others. This nightmare was so realistic and so devastating that you were not completely sure it was just a dream. You never forget that dream, but you are so thankful that you woke up to realize that it was all in your head. How relieved were you?

Just like you, I wanted to wake up. But I had no way to escape.

This cannot be happening to me. Why, God, would you do this to me? Bad things aren't supposed to happen to good people! You believe that, don't you? Don't you??? I wish that was always true, because it would certainly help motivate us to do more of the things we know are right. That concept is so difficult to understand sometimes. How can someone who always cuts corners and never has good intentions ever come out ahead of those who strive to do things the right way? I trust that God has a plan for us all and he uses us in very different ways. We will save ourselves a lot of anguish by not wasting time worrying about others and what they are doing or not doing and refocus on how we can be better every day. Our good deeds will be rewarded in time as long as our intentions are selfless.

Thank goodness no one took medical advice from the 15-year-old that day. I was not granted my escape; I had to endure the scariest moments of my life fully conscious and without my family by my side.

When the paramedics arrived, they rushed me to the ambulance, knowing that every minute lost decreased my chances of survival. As they loaded me into the ambulance, one paramedic carried a small bag.

"What's in the bag?" the other paramedic asked.

"Body parts," he answered bluntly.

Chapter 3:
A Medical Journey

Surgical Masks, Fluorescent Lights

As my parents charged north up U.S. 701, my ambulance pulled into the local hospital. The frenzied shouting of a hundred voices combined to form a muffled roar, and fluorescent ceiling lights and faces obscured by hospital masks dominated my view from the gurney.

This can't be happening to me.

The intensity of the situation frightened me. I had no control over my fate. My only task, I had been told, was to stay awake. I had no choice but to trust that the hospital staff would make the right decisions, but I was 15, had lost a leg, and had no family in the room.

I was scared.

You can take care of yourself, do the right things and do your best to avoid trouble. But there WILL come a time in your life where you don't control your destiny. Your fate will be decided by others. This is a time for faith. Complete, unflinching faith in God. I wish I could say that while I was being wheeled through the emergency department that I turned to God. But I can't say that.

I was consumed by the pain, the fear, the uncertainty of whether I would survive the next hour. But it didn't matter. God blessed me. He blessed the hands of the medical staff. Even when I didn't turn to Him, He took care of me. In hindsight, sometimes it's hard to feel deserving of such grace. But we are all His children. I needed Him more than ever at that moment, and He delivered.

As the chaos swirled around me, the medical staff needed to keep me awake, so I received infant doses of pain medication. The entire medical team wore matching blood-spattered scrubs, like a scene from one of the most graphic ER dramas you could ever imagine. They inserted a 6-inch needle into my chest, and I felt it pierce the skin, through my ribs and lodge in my chest. Every time I was jostled the least bit, I could feel the excruciating touch and the crunch of the bones in my legs rubbing against each other.

By this point, I understood real physical pain. What I didn't realize was that the most painful moment of my life was yet to come.

Junior

As I lie in the ER—blinding lights in my face, flashes of nurses asking me questions, doctors' voices conveying life and death immediacy, excruciating pain from the legs, IVs and other miscellaneous tubes hanging off me like extra appendages—I learned a new word.

Catheter. (I still get that queasy feeling just saying the word.)

I was already in the most severe pain of my life. And then I experienced an even sharper, more gut-wrenching pain. The second I felt it, I nearly exploded off the gurney, and two nurses pounced on my chest to hold me down. I managed to lift my head to see what was causing this agonizing pain, and I was introduced to the evil instrument called the catheter.

Imagine how confusing this is for a 15-year-old boy. My Eagle Scout first aid training included bandages, tourniquets and splints. It did not mention catheters, so let me explain this as tactfully as I possibly can.

This huge man—I'm talking Shaq huge—took what we will refer to, in order to keep this book PG-13, as "Junior" in one hand. And in his other paw was a long, thick tube that I would like to describe as nothing short of a dang garden hose! To make the situation worse, he was mating the two together! You should be thankful this book doesn't have illustrations, but trust me when I tell you, one was not meant to go into the other, gracefully.

This must cease and cease now! "STOP! Please stop. You don't have to do this," I pleaded. "We do need to do this," the nurses exclaimed.

Well that burly devil didn't heed my threats, and he kept pushing. The farther he pushed, the worse the torture became. In my mind, this tortuous procedure was wholly unnecessary—Junior wasn't injured in the accident! Leave him alone!

This might be the only fun thing I have for the rest of my life. Be nice to him.

I have learned since that dreadful day to appreciate what these torture tubes do to help our bodies, but I can't help but wonder why the geniuses at Johns Hopkins haven't come up with a less painful way to access the bladder? There must be another entry point somewhere!

I finally calmed down a little, and the staff was much more concerned about replenishing the blood that was seeping out of my legs than the pain in my "tenders." They were doing their best to keep me alive so that I could be flown to a Level I trauma center for immediate surgery.

A helicopter had been dispatched from Duke University Hospital, and every second was crucial. Blood was still gushing into the bandages around my right leg, and I needed surgery not just to save my leg, but to save my life.

When the helicopter landed at the local hospital, staff frantically wheeled me out of the emergency room.

As I was being wheeled out of the emergency room, people were screaming, "Get out of the way!" I could only see the lights flashing on the ceiling and masked faces all around me, but I could imagine people diving out of the way as we rushed past. In the midst of all of the chaos, I heard something that signaled my first "meant-to-be moment."

You know what I mean, right? Meant-to-be moments are those times when things happen to you or you go through something that really doesn't make much sense but after some time it hits you that it all happened for a reason. Confusing circumstances can leave you unsettled. The pain or heartache you experience feels unjustified. But as time passes, you begin to understand more clearly how those moments may just have been orchestrated to be a teachable moment or even to touch you in a way you could never have imagined.

These life-changing moments are another example of God's power to show up when we least expect it and show his love to us. One of the hardest concepts to believe in is that everything happens for a reason. You may not appreciate these moments at first, but have faith that you can overcome your challenge without a reason to your why. All you can do is trust that God places these meant-to-be-moments in our lives and we must be patient enough to receive them.

This is one of mine.

As I was careening through the hospital, for the first time since the ordeal began, I heard the voices of the two most important people in my life.

My parents yelled my name as they rushed into the emergency room. Had they been five seconds later, they would have missed the opportunity to see me because the staff had no intention of slowing down due to the severity of the situation. Had we made our way to the helicopter pad through another route, they would not have seen me. They scrambled to catch up to my gurney and ran alongside me, holding my hand and kissing me on the forehead telling me, "We love you so much!" They tried their hardest to reassure their terrified son: "Everything is going to be OK. We will see you really soon."

I don't know how much they truly believed their own words, but I really needed to hear them.

The doctor pulled them away and advised them to get back in the car and head to Duke University Hospital. I cannot fathom what was going through their minds and hearts as they helplessly watched their baby boy being whisked away to be treated by another team of strangers in another hospital more than an hour's drive away.

With one last gasp through their tears, Mom and Dad shouted, "We love you!" As they watched the medical team wheel me through the automatic doors, they didn't know if this was the last time they would see me alive.

Have you ever missed the opportunity to say something important to someone? I have. What hurts is when you never get the opportunity to tell them again. Maybe you know someone is hurting inside and needs a word of encouragement, but you are too busy, and you assume you will have the chance later.

I have amazing parents. They never miss an opportunity to show me and my sister Elise that we are loved. Mom showers us with kisses and hugs and tells us she loves us. Dad shows his love through devotion. He always found time to play outside or wrestle with me in the living room no matter how tired he was after a long day of teaching and coaching.

That Sunday morning when I left for the Tucker Lake ski show, my parents and I had no clue of what was going to transpire. Would we have said anything differently that day if we had known? My point is that we never know what life is going to throw at us. Are we seeing a loved one for the last time? We can presume that our kind words or actions to someone in need can wait. Life, however, doesn't wait on us. I beg you to tell those you love how you feel and to reach out to those folks in your life who need you now. Don't miss those opportunities. You can change someone's life with just a few words.

The Little Chopper

Outside on the helipad, the blade thumped overhead, fueling the chaos with noise and wind. The nurse and the pilot began to load me onto the Life Flight Chopper. They paused and started discussing options to the problem at hand. Let me rephrase . . . they were freaking out a little.

A problem? You must be kidding me, right? They can't seem to fit me on this metal hummingbird. *How is this possible?* This isn't a little county fair helicopter. These aircraft were designed specifically to transport patients on stretchers to and from destinations. But my heavily bandaged foot was about the size of a Thanksgiving turkey, and it hit the front dash of the copter every time they tried to slide me in. Because the crew was coming to pick up a 15-year-old boy, the EMS had sent the smaller of the two helicopters.

In a noticeable panic the pilot advised Cindy, the flight nurse, that he would need to call for a bigger chopper. It would only take an additional 20 minutes to arrive. Without hesitation, she yelled above the fray, "If we don't get him on this helicopter right now, he's not going to make it!"

The gravity of that statement impressed upon me how grim the situation really was. Later, I was able to appreciate that Cindy's decisive action probably saved my life.

Outside the helicopter, Cindy crouched down to within inches of my face. They could get me in the helicopter, she said, but it wouldn't be easy. I would have to trust them no matter how scary it was going to be. As she explained her plan to get me safely into the helicopter, I saw the sincerity in her eyes. Her passion and care for my well-being comforted me. I trusted her with my life.

Cindy explained that they would use 8 straps about as thick as seat belts to bind me to the stretcher. Then they would turn it on its side to walk it into the doors of the copter and then turn it back to its original position. It would be scary because I would be staring at concrete with nothing to hold on to and no padding below.

The plan seemed to be the most legitimate chance they had of fitting me in the cockpit. As crazy and terrifying as it sounded, I wasn't in a great position to argue. As we were just about to embark on this grand plan, I blurted out, straight-faced, "Don't worry, if I fall off this stretcher . . . I won't run away!"

Cindy laughed and cried at the same time, releasing some pent-up stress.

Just like Cindy had said, the straps kept me from sliding off the stretcher and crashing onto the concrete. The nurse and pilot wedged me like a puzzle piece into the helicopter. Seconds later, we were in the air, zooming toward a bigger hospital, where an experienced trauma team awaited.

Thousands of feet below, Mac and Pam, my parents, piled into a friend's car for a race up Interstate 40. They hoped that their son would still be alive when they arrived in Durham.

When the helicopter hit the ground at Duke, I was unconscious. The medical staff needed to get me into surgery right away. I was blessed with a renowned surgeon, Dr. John Harrelson, and state-of-the-art facilities, but I still was not doing well. The medical team projected that I had about a 25 percent chance of survival due to the excessive blood loss. To save my life, the doctor and his staff would need to cauterize the arteries and reattach some of the severed veins, nerves and muscles in my right leg.

Doctors estimated that if I did survive, there was a 50 percent chance I would have severe brain damage. They knew how much blood I had lost over the previous couple hours. When the body suffers a traumatic injury, the natural response is that many organs will sacrifice their blood to help heal the injured area. Blood will often leave the organs, including the brain, during similar situations.

I can't imagine the chaos and adrenalin that filled that emergency room on that Sunday afternoon, but I am forever grateful for the care I received.

My parents were still en route from Johnston County when the surgeries began. The terrifying emotions that they must have endured over those next few hours are something I cannot imagine. For 15 years, they had loved me, shaped my moral and ethical values, and guided me to a place where I could make responsible decisions. But as I lay quietly on the operating room table, they were powerless to help me. So, they summoned their only resources—their faith in God and the power of prayer.

Remember, their knowledge of my current condition was limited to that five-second encounter at the other hospital. Knowing that the staff couldn't afford to stop the stretcher because of how dire the situation was, could not have been reassuring. Today, you could be calling, texting and getting GPS directions while riding in a car traveling at 90 mph on I-40. But in 1991, my parents could do nothing but ride along, pray, and stoke the embers of hope that their son would be alive when they reached their destination.

Once they arrived at the hospital, my parents were updated on my condition as the surgeries continued. Each report added another layer of hope until Mac and Pam were finally reassured that their son would live.

The doctors were less optimistic, though, about what my right leg would look like and if it would be able to function enough to walk again.

At Duke, the staff evaluated my partial left leg and, considering the limited technological advancements in prosthetic feet, they determined that cutting the tibia a little shorter would make it the perfect length for a below-knee prosthetic. Leaving some of skin on the underside of the leg and some of the calf muscle, they folded the flap over the sawed bone and stapled it together, giving it the appearance of a baseball seam. The nursing staff fabricated a thick plaster cast over the residual limb to keep the incision protected and to keep the knee joint straight.

Preventing contracture of the knee was the medical reason for the cast, but for me it was also a visual barrier that shielded me from what I wasn't ready to see and deal with.

The Good Leg

Now, about the "good" leg. *And let me warn you, we're about to get a little graphic.*

Remember, when Michael first lifted me out of the water, the right leg was the first to crest. When he saw the exposed bones, he lowered me back into the water. The propeller had snapped the larger of the two lower leg bones about 4 inches below the knee. After the accident, it poked out 3 inches from the skin. The smaller of the two bones was broken in three places and several shards of the fibula were uncovered. The right ankle also took a direct blow, and the bone was crushed. Despite all the bone breaks, the soft tissue damage proved to be the medical team's biggest challenge.

The first of what would eventually be many surgeries on the leg required the supporting structures to be placed back in order. The soft tissue damage made it very difficult for the doctors to put the bones back together. They were limited to a few treatment options and placing the leg in a cast was impossible because of the treatments I needed for the skin, blood vessels and tissue. Because I had so many open wounds, doctors were forced to screw my leg bones into an external fixator. Yes, they literally drilled nine nine-inch stainless steel screws into the tibia, lined up the bones, and then locked them all together with this metal contraption that looked like a torture device from a "Saw" movie! The first time

I saw this shiny, cumbersome contraption sticking out at a 45-degree angle from my leg, I wondered if I would have to lug this thing around forever. Luckily, I had to tolerate it for only 6 weeks.

Doctors also inserted two screws into the outside of my right ankle to help the crushed bones heal in their intended positions. Doctors seemed to be less concerned about the aesthetics of the fibula, a non-weight-bearing bone between the knee and ankle. To this day, that bone under an x-ray appears to be shaped like a Z.

Many years later, I severely sprained my ankle and needed an x-ray. The doctor reading the x-rays had never met me before, so when he carried in my x-rays, he looked horrified! My injury was supposedly just an ankle sprain, but when he saw my disfigured fibula, he was totally confused. I got quite the kick out of relaying the story, and he was relieved to learn that my fibula didn't get so disfigured from an everyday mishap.

The medical staff at Duke was near perfect in their re-engineering of the mangled leg. They took great care in repairing the blood flow and reattaching the muscles. Restoring the function of the nervous system posed some challenges, though. Nerves relay sensation to the brain and give directions to the muscles so that they know what the brain is telling them to do. A leg with healed bones and muscles will not do you much good without direction. Unfortunately, with all of the trauma, surgeries, and lots of drugs it took a couple weeks to really find out how well everything was put back together.

The medical staff at Duke had performed intricate, challenging surgeries proficiently and confidently. The support staff proved to be equally adept at their job. They guided my distraught, panicked parents through the hallways of their nightmare with comforting words and sincerity. Understand that practically every shift of every week of their careers, these workers communicate with family members who are going through the worst days of their lives.

I was lucky to be placed on the Pediatric hall on the 5th floor of the tower. Anyone age 16 or older was placed on an adult wing, where the visitation rules are less lenient. For me, having my family by my side 24/7 was an absolute godsend.

The Mask

Those first couple of weeks were foggy glimpses of walls full of Get-Well cards and balloons, interrupted with debilitating pain followed by very strong medicine. Despite my semi-conscious state, I knew that I was constantly surrounded by family and friends who prayed and kept my parents in positive spirits.

Every day or two, I would undergo debridement. A medical team would clean the exposed leg and remove the dead flesh. It was a tedious, painstaking process that left me longing for the next dose of pain medicine. Once my waiting period was past, I could push a button to get the next dose of morphine. Sometimes, the pain was so excruciating that I left my finger on that button for hours at a time, not wanting to go an extra second before that next hint of relief.

To this day, most people comment about how well I dealt with the pain and the reality of my situation. During those first few days, though, I wasn't dealing with anything. Sure, I downplayed the pain by not complaining or verbalizing it. But I wasn't coherent enough to think about my future, and even if I'd had the notion, I couldn't have been depressed. It was my duty to let those people around me know that their efforts were helping me stay positive.

How was I doing so well emotionally?

I wore a mask. For the first three-and-a-half weeks in the hospital, I wore a mask. Not a Halloween mask, or even an oxygen mask. I wore that false smile that we put on our faces to disguise our true feelings; that permanent half-smile that keeps us from having to deal with our problems.

You have probably worn this mask. You may be wearing it right now. Maybe your life is spiraling out of control. Anxiety is slowly eating at you. Things aren't good at home. Financial burdens are weighing on you. Your guilt and shame for past mistakes are consuming your thoughts. You hate work. Your friends have turned on you. Your addictions control you.

Whatever the reason, you are broken, and you don't want anyone to know about it. So, you don this facade. It's hard to let people into our lives. It's hard to feel vulnerable and ask for help. The mask just seems easier to put on in the hopes that it will all go away.

"I'm OK. I'm fine," you say, hoping that you've fooled your family, friends, and coworkers.

I know this game all too well. I was really, really good at it. I wanted everyone to think that I was OK. And it worked well. My mother on occasion would tell me, "It's OK to be sad. It's OK to be angry. It's OK to cry and let your emotions out."

I remember asking her one day after one of her pleas for me to let it out . . . "Is it OK if I'm fine?" She nodded her head in support, but I know deep down she knew I wasn't being honest with my emotions. She knew I shouldn't be doing this well and handling it the way I was. It wasn't natural. She was afraid that I was going to go crazy one day and lose my mind completely.

To be honest, I had no clue what I was thinking. I hadn't given myself a moment to process or think about what had happened to me. What was my future going to look like? I hadn't had a chance to think lucidly about it since those brief moments on the dock when I begged Michael Pittman to hit me with a paddle and put me out of my misery. The positivity that I displayed so well, for so long, was born from a need to help everyone else before I tried to help myself. I was ignorant to understanding the ramifications of this accident, and too busy with surgeries and company to process it all.

I had the most amazing support you could imagine. Family members, Ski Heels teammates, friends from school, church folks— they all came to visit me at the hospital. Even during the night, I was never alone.

There was a "Sign up to Sleep with Chad" sign on my door! How cool is that? Let me explain, though, before your mind starts to wander in naughty directions. The list held names of aunts and uncles, cousins, and of course, my parents—anyone who wanted to sacrifice a night of comfort to be in my room with me. I was a scared kid in an unfamiliar place who didn't want to face reality. With the constant company around me, I didn't have to.

And for them, I wore that mask.

Through the years I have learned that the "I'm OK mask" has never fixed any problem. But as a 15-year-old lying in a hospital bed and seeing the distress and concern on the faces of the people I love most, I had to make them feel better. And they could only feel better if I pretended that I was OK.

I had one rule that was well known to my family and all that would pay me a visit. My room was a "No-Cry Zone." I asked everyone who entered only one thing: If anyone was going to cry, they had to leave the room. One of my initial reasons for implementing the rule was that I don't recall ever seeing my dad cry before. He was an amazing father who showed my family a great amount of love, but he was the rock, and his bravado held the tears in even in the saddest of moments. My dad was the biggest, strongest man I knew, and he could do and fix anything. I didn't think I could handle seeing my superhero moved to tears. I wanted that strong man there to tell me everything was going to be just fine.

The second reason I wanted the crying ban was that my mother cried at *Steel Magnolias, Beaches, The Fox and the Hound* - she might have even shed a tear during *The Goonies*. I love the fact that she is not afraid to show her emotions, but I didn't want to see her constantly upset. Most kids are afraid of doing two things to their parents, disappointing them and upsetting them. I wanted positive energy and that included all of my visitors.

Some friends on their visit to see me didn't know how to act, what to say. Even "How are you doing?" turned from a breezy everyday greeting to a sincere question grounded in pity. Sometimes, I would break the ice by asking a friend to scratch an itch in my missing foot. They'd scratch the air, and believe it or not, I felt a sensation of relief. The phantom sensations of pain and itching are mysterious, but they are very real.

The ones who lifted my spirits the most were the ones who asked me if I had seen the highlights on ESPN or if I thought the N.C. State Wolfpack would be any good this year. They were the ones who made me feel like I was still the same person, regardless of how many screws were sticking out of my disfigured right leg and regardless of how much of my left leg had been sawed off. You always will have a couple of those great friends that no matter the situation you are in, they still crack jokes with you or crawl in the bed with you and watch the movie without saying a word. I was truly blessed.

Celebrity appearances

My story became a media sensation, long before millions of people were watching viral videos on YouTube and Facebook. I slurred my way through a couple of television interviews, the pain medicine exaggerating my Robeson County drawl and furthering the stereotype of the slow-speaking country boy. Many newspapers across the state were running articles and calling for interviews. We were on a wild ride, mixed with emotions of hurt, pain, thankfulness, grief, love and anxiety.

People were certainly interested in this tragic story.

The TV coverage sparked an avalanche of letters, cards and flowers from well-wishers. I didn't know many of the senders, and my parents didn't know some of them either. Soon, cards started flowing in from North Carolina royalty—University of North Carolina basketball coach Dean Smith, Duke Coach Mike Krzyzewski, and even Senator Jesse Helms. N.C. State basketball star Chris Corchiani called to chat with me a few times. Twenty years later, I came into contact with Corchiani and told him how awesome it was that he had taken the time to call me. He said he remembered the accident and our conversations.

Each one of those Carolinians made an impact by reaching out to one 15-year-old boy with a devastating injury. But, for me, they were all dwarfed by Jim Ritcher.

Ritcher, an N.C. State lineman and Outland Trophy winner who started in four Super Bowls with the Buffalo Bills, stopped by the hospital to bring me a Super Bowl football. In person! Jim and the Bills had just come off their second consecutive loss in the Super Bowl, and before he headed back to training camp, he came to Duke to see me!

But as fate would have it, I was comatose. And when he found out that I was too drugged up to receive visitors that day, he said he would come back later.

A nice gesture, sure. But what NFL Pro Bowler has time to visit a kid in the hospital twice?

When I came to realize what had transpired that day, to say I was disappointed would be a severe understatement. I certainly appreciated his kindness but was a little heartbroken that I had missed an opportunity to meet a Wolfpack hero and an All-Pro football player.

A couple days later, I looked up from my bed to see this imposing figure blocking the entire doorway. You guessed it; Jim Ritcher had returned. He gave me his undivided attention for several minutes, he encouraged me, and put that rare football in my hands.

If ever there was a reason for a kid to idolize a pro athlete, Jim Ritcher was it! Though I am not star-struck these days, when you see someone giving their time so selflessly, it always earns my utmost respect.

How often do we hear the terms hero and role model thrown around today? Our kids idolize sports figures and celebrities; they look up to them, listen to them, and watch them on social media. Kids emulate their best moves. Even adults admire people who have certain things or look a certain way. We imagine they have more money, more fame and fewer troubles. But beauty, fame, and wealth aren't the attributes that deserve our adulation.

In adulthood, I have matured to admiring individuals who serve others with a selfless and generous heart—helping and giving to others without expecting any recognition.

We all love to be recognized for our good deeds, but when we choose to serve and help others without expecting anything in return, our payment becomes so much richer. Like Jim Ritcher, who came to visit this 15-year-old kid, without the press, without the cameras, long before social media. He did it because he wanted to make a difference. He did it because he knew how blessed he was in life, and that maybe he could help improve someone else's situation. He made an impact on a teenage boy and his family that day. I'm sure he didn't realize how much his visit would resonate with me even as an adult.

I try my best to include my children in the philanthropic work that I am involved in. I want my kids to choose to emulate me as their role model. I want them to see what giving back can mean to others. Give selflessly and I guarantee that the return to you will be tenfold.

Chapter 4:
Facing the Future

Painful Reality

About three weeks after the accident, some of the biggest medical hurdles were behind me. Doctors had finally covered up all the open wounds with skin grafts that they harvested from my upper thigh. The skin was secured in place with about a hundred staples. This meant I could start weaning off the heavy pain meds. As the fog lifted from my brain, I could more clearly see my future. I would live the rest of my life as an amputee. I had never met an amputee, so I had no concept of the everyday struggles I might face. My primary concern was that I might never play sports again or even be able to continue any kind of active lifestyle.

I had been, as modestly as a 15-year-old kid could possibly put it, a great athlete. I had been one of the best basketball players in my school. I was MVP of the football team. And I had scored almost every one of my football team's touchdowns in ninth grade—as a tight end. I was a lock to play on the varsity team as a sophomore, and college scouts already had their eyes on me. I had no doubt that I would be suiting up the pads on Saturdays and one day in the NFL on Sunday afternoons.

Those dreams ended in an instant at Tucker Lake, and I wondered if I could ever play competitive sports at any level ever again.

In an effort to lift my spirits, a physical therapist scheduled an appointment to show me an inspirational video. She held the VHS tape up like a trophy and described it to me as "life-changing." This video, she said, features amputees playing basketball, just like I was used to playing. She had my attention! My athletic dreams were still alive, and this video would prove it. This was going to change my life forever.

That video did inspire me, but in a way the PT could never have imagined.

With the room full of family, friends, and staff, the nurse pushed the tape into the video player. I processed it very quickly.

I'm not sure if you are familiar with the phrase "bless your heart" that we frequently use in the South, so let me explain. You can say something that may not be that positive about someone, but if you follow that up with "bless your heart," it softens the insult. Like, "Did you see Judy's new haircut? Bless her heart!" (Judy's haircut was a hot mess.) I'm not condoning it, but it's just what's done.

I saw men with artificial legs shuffling around, shooting basketball, barely jumping, missing shots, and looking like they could be competitive—against an elementary school team.

Bless their hearts for trying.

But I was devastated.

This was a cruel look at what my future might be. The realization that I might never walk or play sports again was devastating. To me, the video had been more of a demonstration of what I couldn't do than what I could do. My future enjoyment of sports had been in doubt, and that video answered my questions with a resounding "No!"

Was this video what I had to look forward to? This was the best I could hope for? They made a video of these guys, so they must be the superstars. They are the best one-legged athletes they could find.

Then it hit me! I don't even have one good leg! The chances of me even being as good as they were is extremely doubtful.

I couldn't bear to watch another second.

"You can take it out now," I directed the physical therapist. I couldn't put into words what I was feeling. Still wearing my mask and with the intentions of not causing a scene, I hid my emotions as best that I could.

The Worst Day Ever!

I was devastated. For the first time since having my life turned upside down, I cried.

I clearly recall thinking; I will never play sports again if that is what I am going to look like. I am not going to be one of those guys hobbling around the court and hearing people praise me for my courage, but not my ability. I don't want to play for hugs.

I told everyone to leave the room, that I wanted to be alone.

Grief, anger and self-pity overwhelmed me. I had no more strength to maintain the facade. For the first time, there was nobody in the room who needed me to be strong.

False bravado had trapped three weeks' worth of pain, anguish and tears deep down in my gut. I'd worn a mask of invincibility for my mom, my sister, my friends, my Ski Heels teammates, and the reporters who came to interview me. I'd had to make them believe that I believed everything would be OK. Alone for the first time, I had no reason to wear my mask. My defenses were stripped away.

All I had ever done was try to be a good kid, and yet everything I wanted was being taken away. At 15, I started to think I had nothing to live for anymore. I would never have the things I wanted in life. I would never step back on an athletic field or court again.

I guess I should have been happy to be alive. I should have been satisfied to have another day on this earth because things could have easily turned out differently. But I had just seen my best future on a VHS tape, and I was not feeling grateful.

So, I cried. Angrily, violently, justifiably, I cried. A tearful mixture of self-pity and rage soaked my pillow. For the first time, the gravity of my loss spilled out of me in an emotional meltdown.

Remember that sign-up sheet to sleep with Chad? In a month-long calendar filled with the names of family and friends, there was one blank spot. And it was this night. I was all alone. I was finally forced to focus on my own thoughts, to process the entire situation.

My heart and brain had been battered by gloom and uncertainty. The day of the accident was certainly a terrible day. But on this day, I had lost all hope, and that was more crippling than losing my leg. This was the worst day ever. And I was all alone.

I just wanted to be out of this nightmare; I wanted it to be over! I didn't want the pain anymore. I felt like my life was no longer worth living. I probably would have taken my life that night had I been able to get out of the bed and find the device to do it.

For some reason, not one nurse opened my door to check on me the entire night. Every other night I couldn't go 30 minutes without being poked or prodded, but on this night, I was locked in a room with nothing but my pillow, my blanket and my desperate thoughts. Call me crazy, but something strange was happening. The video. Hope lost. Empty slot on the sleeping list. No medical intervention all night. Something was happening.

I believe in my heart that these strange occurrences were no coincidence. They all were happening on the same day for a divine purpose. This was another Meant to Be Moment.

The Voice

If I was going to survive another day, I needed answers. I needed a concrete understanding of all that was happening to me.

I clenched my pillow, half soaked with tears and sweat, and I asked the questions once, and then a thousand more times, "Why me? Am I being punished for something? What on earth could I have done to deserve this?"

Sure, I had a few marks against me. I pulled the chair out from under Matthew Fritz in science class and he had to be taken to the hospital to get stitches. There were times when I might not have been the best little brother in the world. But I had done my share of good deeds, too. I walked my mom's special needs students to their buses and helped them at Special Olympics. I had just received my Eagle Scout Award. I was heavily involved in my family's church—I was literally a choir boy! And after all that I'd done to try to live by the Word, God failed me. He did this to me. He allowed this to happen.

Just a month prior to the accident, I had given myself to God. On a warm spring evening, I found myself sitting in the concrete bleachers of Lumberton High School's football stadium.

Admittedly, I wasn't there to hear God's word. I was there to talk to girls. Some of the cutest girls in town were going, so I rode over to the stadium with some buddies.

Despite my less-than-noble intentions, I was meant to be there that night. The stadium was hosting a revival, and the speaker was testifying to the city's youth. Huge, thumping speakers rocked the stadium as a band played Christian tunes that helped to get us energized for the message. The youthful spirit in the stadium bleachers infused me with a much different feeling than I got sitting in a pew at church on Sunday morning.

I was in a sea of middle and high school kids, soaking up a powerful message about how Jesus wants to be our friend, and how he wants a relationship with us. I knew a lot of Bible stories and rarely missed a Sunday morning service, but for some reason, that speaker at the youth rally reached me, and I felt something more. Before I knew what was happening, he asked us if we wanted to have a relationship with God. And if we did, he asked us to walk down onto that football field. Before I realized that my feet were moving, the Spirit had propelled me down the steps with dozens of other teenagers. I didn't really understand why I was going down there or what I expected to happen, but I went anyway. We all took a knee on that dew-covered grass and said a prayer together.

I don't remember the exact words that I spoke that night, but it felt good. I was told I was saved. I'm now Jesus' main man! We officially have this relationship that can never be broken.

But I felt much different that night in the hospital room. I felt despondent, enraged, betrayed.

Why me? I asked You into my life to be my personal savior and trusted that you would always be there for me no matter what. Why? Why did you do this to me?

The Man upstairs was getting an earful.

Is this your grand plan for me? Did you make this boat run over me? Is this your plan for the kid who gave his life to you on that football field?

Why me?

It's hard to explain what happened next in my hospital room. The lights in my room stopped buzzing, the machines stopped blinking and the traffic on the street below faded away.

There was a second of pure concentrated silence as I stared at the ceiling through a salty, watery blur.

"Don't worry. You'll find out."

I don't know if I heard it with my ears or my soul. But I distinctly heard those words that night.

"Don't worry. You'll find out."

There was no question in my mind that it was God talking to me. If I had been speaking to myself, I wouldn't have been that vague. I would have given very clear details of why and what to expect next. Maybe even a timeline.

But God demands trust and patience.

"Don't worry. You'll find out."

I waited and begged to hear more answers, a real explanation. But the room remained silent. Even as I longed for clarity and justification, peace filled the room. I stopped crying. I thought about all the times in Bible School and from Pastor Sam when I'd heard stories about what God does for us. For some reason, that's all I needed to hear that night.

As I lay alone in that bed, hope crept back into my life.

It's hard to understand and appreciate hope until you have lost it. Until you have hit rock bottom and there isn't an ounce left inside you, you will never comprehend its power. Hope is what keeps us going when we don't understand why. Physically, I still didn't have anything to look forward to. God hadn't miraculously healed my leg. Logically, nothing had changed. One leg was mangled, and the other was half gone. So, why did my tears dry up?

Love and faith.

I felt God's love in those words. And that supplied me with the faith that I could still control how I adapted to my situation. That night, I understood that the accident had happened for a reason. I didn't know I would help inspire others to do great things or that I would touch the lives of people all across the country. I only knew that God was with me, and that gave me the strength to fight.

I made a conscious decision that night to see what was possible. I wanted to find out how good Chad could be.

At certain moments in our lives, we find ourselves at a crossroads—a time when we make decisions that will significantly shape our future. I found myself facing the hardest decision of my life. Each one of us has faced, is facing, or will face challenges that feel insurmountable. It's hard to imagine how you will ever get past it. These are the exact moments that create the strongest of the strong.

No matter what you are going through, your choices will be narrowed to a couple of options. Give up or fight! You might see it as more complicated than that, but ultimately that's what it comes down to. Quitting is easy, my friend. Just give up and let your problem defeat you. The other option is to fight, and fighting is much more difficult. It takes courage and strength. Fighting requires effort. It requires faith.

When I considered my future as an amputee, I wanted to quit. I wanted to end it all. I had nothing to look forward to. Maybe you know exactly how that feels.

I had a supportive family and a great upbringing. I know that's not the case for everyone. I had a foundation of faith that helped me. I know that isn't the situation for everyone. So those who are faced with a tough circumstance and don't have those things to fall back on ... do they have a pass to roll over and give up?

No, Ma'am! No, Sir!

Even with those foundational supports on my side, I had no reason to keep fighting. I couldn't imagine anything positive resulting from my accident. Therefore, why in the heck would I give the effort to fight?

I had a vital decision to make. And this decision forever changed the course of my life.

As hard as it was to believe that things would ever be OK again, I chose to fight. I made the conscious decision to give every ounce of my energy to every miniscule improvement. I couldn't yet see a bright future with a great job, a beautiful family and a chance to impact so many others' lives. I only saw the next weight to push, the next step to take and the next obstacle to overcome.

I am so happy I did not give up. Trust me when I tell you that I know what it feels like to not see past the darkness. I know what it feels like to see no future. I saw no silver lining. But I did trust that my God would not give up on me no matter how bad it seemed.

Whatever is weighing you down, whatever is eating you alive, or whatever mountain stands in front of you, as long as you have a breath in you, you have a chance. You are worthy, and you owe it to yourself to fight. Giving up is NOT an option when you realize that you deserve better.

I refused to let the loss of my leg define who I was going to become. I was not then, and I am not now, a quitter. I will fight.

The next day, I gave every ounce of effort I could muster to every challenge from the medical staff. I was determined to realize my true potential through hard work, dedication, and faith.

One short-term goal was to use the bathroom on my own, so I could get this garden hose pulled out of Junior. To do so, I needed to regain the strength in my abdominals, so when the therapists asked me to exercise my core, I did everything they asked and more, if they would let me. They built a steel contraption over my bed with a triangle handle attached to a chain that allowed me to pull my body up and start to build some upper body strength. After losing 35 pounds, almost exclusively muscle tone, every attempt at exercising was quickly met with exhaustion and lightheadedness. But it wouldn't stop me.

You need to understand that I never loved working out. I would do all of the repetitions, and I would push myself to do more than my teammates. I was motivated by tangible results—success in sports. For some people, finding the motivation to live healthy through exercise and diet comes easy. For others like me, it's a lifetime battle. I was never eager to visit the weight room, and I prefer cheeseburgers to salads every time. I also don't love running. I run for only a few reasons . . . a masked man with a chainsaw is chasing me, my dog has slipped through the fence and is headed for the South Carolina border, or there is a ball involved on a court or field. That's pretty much it.

Sitting in the hospital, I pondered how much things had changed. There were no promises of sports success to motivate me. And if I were cast in a chainsaw horror movie, I would be the first victim.

But with Mom's encouragement and Dad's relentlessness to keep me focused, I gradually built my endurance. I ached to be able to do any of the things I used to do. I was so limited that I began to look forward to going to the hospital "gym." It was slightly larger than a patient room and included a set of stairs, a therapy table, a few weighted balls, and some therapy bands. Dad would unload me and my casted stump and steel-infused leg onto the mats, and we would push some weight. It was deflating to see how bony I had become. Before, I was bone and muscle. After three weeks at Duke, I was skin and bone. But we pressed forward, concentrating on more weight and more repetitions each time.

My dad taught me to stay in the present and work with what I have. The past cannot be changed. The now is all that matters. I was determined more than ever to give this new life a fighting chance.

It wasn't easy to change my outlook. I didn't want to relearn how to stand or walk or get in and out of the bed safely. It took every ounce of strength to stay positive every time I failed, especially when the task would have been simple in my previous life.

My expectations were so low. My fight grew every day, but I struggled to visualize a great life ahead. It's hard to see past your own shadow sometimes. It's hard to get excited about a life you never wanted.

But I was determined. This was not the mask of optimism I had worn in front of family and friends for so long. No! This was a different outlook, grounded in reality and built on determination and faith.

Instead of trying to reach an ultimate goal that wasn't even on the horizon yet, I looked at the road directly in front of me and took small steps. I focused on the immediate future and what I could control at that particular moment. Every step, every small accomplishment allowed me to move forward.

Zig Ziglar put it very eloquently, "Go as far as you can see, and you will see farther. You don't have to be great to start, but you have to start to be great."

Just fight. Do what you can now to start your journey toward your goal. Baby steps are OK, but keep leaning forward.

Influences at Duke

During my stay at Duke, I met many people who encouraged and consoled me and my family. From doctors and nurses, to friends and strangers, they all played a significant role in my journey. Over my month-long stay in the hospital, I met a couple of people I will never forget.

The first was my main doctor, John Harrelson. His combination of knowledge and experience was unrivaled, but he was still as down to earth as any doctor has ever been. He wasn't exactly *Patch Adams* silly, but his sense of humor accentuated by his frightening resemblance to Notre Dame football coach Lou Holtz made him the perfect MD for me.

I remember one day he visited for his daily rounds, and my room was packed with friends. Instead of asking everyone to leave so he could evaluate and counsel me, he came right on in as if the party was for him.

At this time, the medical staff was extremely concerned about the motor function of the right leg. I wasn't able to lift my foot, and Dr. Harrelson checked its progress on every visit. No matter what he said, and no matter how hard I tried, I just couldn't lift that foot. As I lay on the bed in front of my friends, Dr. Harrelson put me through the routine again, and the result didn't change—my foot didn't move.

Then this orthopedist pulled a lighter out of his scrub jacket and brandished it like a magician's prop. My friends became silent and some even concerned as he kept demanding that I pull the foot up! I mustered my strength and tried again, but the foot stayed in place.

With a scrape of his thumb across the lighter, Dr. Harrelson created fire. My friends' mouths dropped open as he placed the burning lighter under my foot.

"Now, can you lift your foot, Chad?" Dr. Harrelson asked, as if he was going to use the heat from the flame to force my foot to cooperate. As the flame inched closer to the tender bottom of my foot, one of my best friends, Heath Stone, rose from his chair, his shoulders back and his chest puffed out. His eyes were fixed on Dr. Harrelson and the flame under my foot. This country boy had seen enough, and he planned to end this torture session. Dr. Harrelson saw Heath coming, quickly extinguished the flame, and disarmed the young man with a wide grin and a hearty laugh.

Everyone in the room who had ever met this amazing doctor knew he was just teasing, but the few who hadn't met him must have thought he was insane. One thing was confirmed that day—Heath Stone was a good friend. Not everyone is willing to tackle a doctor for you!

The gags and hijinks were part what made Dr. Harrelson so impactful to me. And his hugs and encouragement helped my parents survive some of the most trying days of their lives. Duke is indeed fortunate to have had this man on staff as a healer and a professor for more than 60 years.

Another huge influence on me during those few weeks on the pediatric floor was a young baseball pitcher named Shane Coltrain. Because Shane and I were both young athletes who had lost a limb, we immediately bonded.

Shane's incident was so bizarre. You might expect that somebody who has been chopped up by a propeller might lose a leg. But Shane's need for amputation was entirely unexpected. His life was changed when he was hit in the leg by a baseball—something that happens to every kid whoever picks up a glove. After getting hit, Shane got sick, then deathly ill. A staph infection entered his body, and before doctors could put their finger on the source of what was making him so sick, it was too late. They had to make the decision to remove his leg above the knee in order to save his life. The infection not only killed the viable cells in his leg, but it caused astronomical swelling. The buildup in fluid was so severe and so rapid that his skin could stretch no thinner and started to split.

Like me, Shane required skin grafts, but mine were minimal compared to the amount of skin that had to be replaced all over Shane's body. Both he and his family were strong believers and as with me, they found strength to fight through this horrible endeavor. During our time at Duke, Shane and I compared injuries, discussed treatments, and shared our feelings about how our lives had changed. He fed me with strength, and I'd like to think I was able to do the same for him.

Shane is still inspiring many people today. He now helps other amputees realize their true potential by building state-of-the-art prosthetics. His passion for his patients and his understanding of how hard it is to start life all over again shines through him with everyone he encounters. He is another testament to how good God is when you lean on him to help you through those tough times.

Chapter 5: Homecoming

Overwhelming Support

My time on the fifth floor at Duke Hospital neared its end, and I would be going home for a few weeks before coming back for rehabilitation. I felt relieved but also very nervous. I had made friends with the staff and had grown comfortable in this safe setting with the best in the medical industry at my beck and call. The thought of heading to a familiar setting, where I'd be able to sleep in my own bed, pet my dog, and eat my mom's cooking every day should have been motivational and joyous. But I wasn't sure that my family and I were ready for the challenges my going home could bring.

When I was discharged from Duke. I had lost virtually all strength in my upper body; my shoulder was banged up and I had stitches in my thumb. Plus, I had Frankenstein's leg on one side and a nub on the other. I was a freak show, a curiosity. For once, I understood what it felt like to be self-conscious and dependent.

I cautiously slid my lanky butt into that faux-wood paneled station wagon and headed down I-40 and 95 south to good ol' Robeson County. As we turned down the street I had lived on for my entire life, I noticed cars parked on the street—dozens of cars.

My family and friends had organized a surprise, welcome home party. But I wasn't sure I was ready for this. I had butterflies in my stomach as badly as I had experienced in playing my first T-ball game as a 4-year-old. I was happy to see half the town, but I wasn't ready to be put on display quite yet. Shaving cream on the driveway spelled out "Welcome Home Chad" and a sea of friends and neighbors applauded as the wagon pulled in. Mixed emotions flooded my soul. I didn't know if I should cry out of joy or anxiety.

As I slid backwards into the bulky wheelchair, guarding those five metal contraptions protruding from my right leg, my frisky black Lab Suzy greeted me. With a balloon tied from her collar, she danced around the chair with excitement. It's amazing to me how keen animals can be. This 90-pound lap dog loved to jump all over you and wash your face with her kisses. Yet, during the next few weeks, she approached me calmly and gently. All without being told.

The one part of the party I was excited about was the food. In North Carolina, it's not a party unless there's a bunch of good ol' boys standing around some meat being cooked over an open flame. The smell of the grill in the open air certainly trumped the hospital food I'd been eating for weeks.

But the atmosphere was just awkward. People were being nice— too nice. They'd see the carnage of my legs, and they'd feel pity and sense the need to comfort me. They tried to make me feel better, but what I needed was normalcy. Less attention. Fewer concerned looks. Fewer earnest attempts at encouragement. I just wanted things to feel normal, and I wondered if they ever would be.

My friends wanted to be there to welcome me and lift my spirits. But just as I couldn't imagine what life would be like after losing a leg, most of my peers didn't know how to greet me when they truly believed that my life was ruined.

Fortunately, I also had some pretty awesome friends. While the grownups were carefully saying all the right things and being annoyingly polite, my friends started teasing me and laughing with me and treating me like Chad. And that was what I needed.

For the two and a half weeks I was home, my life was fairly miserable. Most of the kids my age were out playing ball and swimming and fishing and enjoying what was left of their summer. I had my family and my dog and occasional visits from my friends, but I spent my best days in a wheelchair, the worst in my bed.

Mom and Dad became pseudo-nurses, changing dressings and cleaning my grisly wounds. They cared for me and comforted me with undying love.

As much as I enjoyed being in my own room, I was anxious to get back to Duke and start rehab. I didn't really know what to expect, but I was determined to do whatever I could. The unknown can be very scary, especially when we like to control our situations. That's where faith has to step in. I could only trust that there would be a better tomorrow.

Screws and Staples

When I got to Duke South to begin my rehab, doctors removed all the screws from my right leg. I assumed that this would be a highly intricate surgery, but boy was I wrong! They literally hooked up a Black & Decker drill to my screws and backed them out one by one.

Now that the bones were aligned well enough and the skin grafts had healed, the medical staff began removing the 200-plus staples. I remember that ordeal explicitly! Sharp, pointy wire cutters snipped the center of each staple, and then needle nose pliers pulled each individual shard. Most of the staples slid out easily, but some clung to patches of skin like a tick on a dog's back. With enough twisting and tugging, all the staples were eventually ripped out.

Finally, I thought. *I'm free! Take me to rehab. I'm ready to start strengthening this leg.*

Wrong.

The leg wasn't fully healed so the doctors slapped on a cast that started at my toes and ended just short of my earlobes. Ok . . . maybe that's a slight exaggeration, but it was so far up into my thigh region that it was impossible to poop without a suitcase to prop up my ankle! When they finished, it felt like my leg was encased in 100 pounds of cement.

Next came my first prosthesis, the fake left leg that I would learn to walk on.

I had no clue what to expect, but I was ready to get back on my feet, even if one of them was artificial. When the medical team pulled out the new prosthesis, it bore no resemblance to an actual leg. It was just a hard, open-ended casting with a rubber foot on the end. But that was OK. Compared to the tree trunk that was my right leg, the prosthesis was barely a concern. I had to slip on a pantyhose fabric to cut down on the friction, and little nub-shaped socks added some padding.

Once I slipped my leg inside the hard mold and clipped in the top lip, I was ready for a monumental moment—Standing!

My mom pointed the video camera in my direction, and my dad held a prayer in his throat. My grandmother—parked against the wall in her wheelchair—crossed her fragile fingers, hoping that I'd be successful. My face demonstrated a fire and determination to show them all what I was made of. Mario, my physical therapist, had his belt around my waist to ensure I would not collapse to the ground. With my dad by my side, I held myself up on the parallel bars with my skinny arms and dropped my weight onto my hobbled legs.

And for the first time since I'd lost my leg to a propeller in Tucker Lake, I stood.

My atrophied arms shaking as they tried to relieve the pressure on the legs, I lasted about 20 seconds before the blood rushed to my lower extremities and I got light-headed. But I had stood.

Then came Round 2. This time I lifted that artificial leg with my hip muscles and used my thigh muscles to straighten out my knee. Gently lowering that rubber heel to the floor, I shifted my weight over to it and hiked my right hip up enough to swing that massive cast forward to meet up with its partner. I had just taken a step!

I had to consciously think about each movement in perfect sequence in order to make it happen, but I was walking. After just a couple of steps, I was thoroughly exhausted.

It was the most daunting physical challenge I'd ever encountered. Endless burpees during the final hour of two-a-day football practices, exhausting suicides at the end of a grueling basketball practice— nothing I had ever done compared to the challenge of those first steps.

And that was as far as I got during that first day of rehab—a couple of steps.

Just six weeks earlier, I had been a strapping young athlete, water skiing around a lake in a gorilla suit. But six weeks of immobility can be devastating to the body. As excited as everyone was that I was temporarily back on my feet, I quickly realized that there was no elevator to normalcy. I was going to have to take the hard road to accomplish these goals. But I was determined.

I was scheduled to spend two-and-a-half weeks at Duke South, but I walked out (with crutches) in ten days. During that brief time, I encountered some of the most inspiring people I've ever met.

Mountains of Courage

One day between physical therapy sessions, I was lying in the room alone half-watching TV as my eyelids inched closer and closer together. Out of the corner of my eye I saw some movement just outside my door. What I saw was so low to the ground that I wondered if someone had brought a service animal to the floor, or if a child had scampered by. Or maybe, I thought, the strength of my medication was causing me to hallucinate. I had almost forgotten about it until I saw the miniature shadow again. More curious than sleepy, I maneuvered myself into the wheelchair and pushed myself to the doorway to investigate.

I was astonished by what I saw when I reached the hallway. A lady in her 70s had lost both legs above the knee, had lost one arm and four fingers on her remaining hand. But she refused to stop walking.

Every day, she walked up and down the hall repeatedly on her stumps with little pads on them for comfort. When I finally saw her clearly for the first time, I was drawn to her smile, her aura, her attitude. As I got to know her, I learned her story. She had been a rugged, healthy mountain woman. Her problems started with a common tick bite. She had always treated illnesses with home remedies and did everything she could to avoid the hospital. But her plants and herbs were no match for Rocky Mountain Spotted Fever. By the time she admitted that she needed medical help, her life was in danger. The doctors were forced to remove her limbs just to save her life.

Like me, she had done nothing wrong to deserve such a gloomy fate. Somehow, though, she didn't feel sorry for herself. She lost both legs and an arm, but she didn't lose her spirit.

If there was ever a reason for me to push myself to take one more step or do one more repetition with the dumbbells, here she was, shuffling down the hall and smiling at the nurses, the cleaning crew, total strangers.

I never saw her look unhappy. She was always laughing, engaging and talking to everybody. That was a very powerful message to me. Any time I needed extra motivation, I thought of this beautiful lady, her perseverance and her infectious attitude.

If she can do this, I thought, there's nothing I can't do.

These are the moments that help put life back into perspective. Poor me. Why am I having to deal with all of this? Nobody understands what I am going through. No one knows the pain I am experiencing. I thought my accident was one of the worst things in the world. I had moments of self-pity, moments of wanting to give up.

But for me it was extremely humbling to see others who had been through so much and still be encouraged by their strength. Be careful not to compare your situation with others, but pull strength from those who have endured great trials.

Chapter 6:
An Unfamiliar Experience

Burning Stares

I left Duke with my temporary new leg and a pair of crutches with towels taped around the top to protect my pits. I was out of sorts for the remainder of the summer. I couldn't be with the Ski Heels, I couldn't work out with the football team, I couldn't work out in the weight room. Most of the summer was gone.

I had to prepare for the new school year, and I was terrified. I used to be excited to head back to see all of my friends that I had missed while we had lived at the lake during the summer. I had never been anxious about going back to school ... well, except on those occasions that I had forgotten to study for a test or complete a project. But this was a different type of anxiety.

In the fall, two other schools were scheduled to merge with my school, Lumberton Senior High School. The influx of new faces concerned me. I wouldn't be the Eagle Scout, the athlete, the class president. The students only knowledge of me would be "The Guy Who Lost His Leg." That's what I had to look forward to for my sophomore year.

Unlike previous school years, I didn't have weeks of football practice behind me when I walked—limped, hobbled, struggled—through the doors on the first day of school. I had missed all of the bonding, the joking, the camaraderie, the pain, the growth that came with weeks of football practice—sometimes twice a day—under the relentless Carolina sun.

For the first time, I wasn't part of it.

I didn't belong.

Because my right leg was in a cast all the way up to my hip, I had to wear shorts to school every day, leaving my unrealistic prosthetic leg fully exposed. Luckily, I had progressed to where I didn't have to use crutches. Instead, I leaned on my grandfather's cane that he whittled from a tree root. This connection to my family gave me strength, but it didn't improve my status in the image-conscious world of high school. Every hallway was full of socially conscious teenagers comparing their new hairdos, their new jeans, their new T-shirts.

I was the only one with a new leg.

And it was exposed. Naked. I only wanted to blend in and be normal.

The burning stares of a hundred teenagers melted right through my robotic extension of a leg. They looked the other way until I passed, but nearby conversations drifted off to peculiar silence and the pushing, shoving and jostling of a high school hallway came to a conspicuous halt.

Most of the students had never seen a one-legged person, let alone someone their own age. Their gawking could be excused. At the other end of the spectrum, some kids tried too hard to help. I translated their good intentions as pity, and that was almost as painful as the emergency-room catheter.

I didn't ask for any special provisions. Every time I struggled to open a door or walk down the steps, I was making myself stronger and declaring my independence.

Once I had made some progress, it was finally time to have my hip-high cast removed.

My leg had been in the cast for weeks, so as the technician sawed the cast down to the cotton padding, we all smelled the stench of a high school football locker room after an early August practice.

And the sight was as horrific as the smell. I had almost forgotten how disfigured my leg was because the cast had masked it for so long. The indentations were accentuated by the bumpy ridges of calcified knots of healed bone. The grafts of skin had taken pretty well, but they left a waffle pattern on my leg. When surgeons stripped the skin away from my upper thigh to transplant to the lower leg, it became slick and a little shiny. I felt no sensation in the smooth skin, and the color didn't match that well with the surrounding skin. The five puncture holes from the external fixator were clearly visible, as well as the long scar lines, outlined with staple holes.

The cast had been a pain in the butt, but at least nobody had to look at my disfigured leg. The stares and remarks had not really lessened very much, and I wasn't looking forward to a renewed round of gawking, pointing, and pitying.

There was no normalcy for me. I spent my after-school hours enduring physical therapy at the local gym while my friends were joking around, slapping football pads and enjoying the animalistic pregame rituals of a high school locker room on Friday night.

As painful as it was, my physical therapy time every day after school was actually welcomed. I didn't enjoy the torture and the struggle of rehabbing, but I was in a non-threatening environment where they saw me as Chad and not a spectacle. Kathy Hansen, my therapist, was an amazing woman and the biggest pain in my rear end.

I'm not sugarcoating this. We spent hours upon hours in that small rehab facility. The doctors wanted us to continue trying to free up the nerves in the lower right leg to see if there was any way to regain function in the front of the foot. That poor woman deeply massaged those scars every day hoping for progress.

She also had the task of bringing some movement back into my right knee, which had been virtually straight for over three months. Once a joint gets locked up, it's a feat to get it to bend as normal.

My least favorite exercise was lying on my back with my foot on the wall. I would have to slowly crawl my foot down the wall until the angle of the knee became excruciating, and then she would block the foot from going back up! I had to bite my lip or a towel and suffer through it until the joint broke free. And then I had to drop it farther. These were the cruel and unusual punishments that I endured for months and months.

I thought back to Shane Coltrain and the mountain lady walking on her stumps, and I vowed I would never give up no matter how many tears I shed.

I will find out how amazing I will become. I will not give up.

These moments challenge your faith the most, and giving up seems like the best and easiest option. But these moments reveal our true character. Giving up is easy, but the most rewarding moments are when you fight hard to get what you want. The pride in accomplishment is powerful. We all have unique gifts and are designed for amazing things. Life will never be free of heartache and pain, but you must believe that as long as you have a breath, you have a chance. You can beat whatever you are going through.

We just need a little help sometimes, and it's OK to ask for it.

We resist help because we feel vulnerable. But admitting that you need help is a courageous act that yields positive results. Think about how you feel after you've helped someone who truly needed you. It's a gift to let another person feel that same sense of worth and satisfaction.

I can tell you with absolute certainty that I could have never overcome my circumstances without the help and support of others, especially the ones like Kathy, who enjoyed torturing me on a daily basis, all to make life possible again.

But you must also help yourself. Chin up. Suck it up. Quit feeling sorry for yourself. Fight. You deserve to win!

A New Season

As soon as football season ended, my friends laced up their Air Jordans and started practicing their 3-point shots, post moves and crossover dribbles. I was still trying to strengthen my body, improve my coordination and balance, and regain my independence. This was a rough time for me. Missing football was one thing because I was still injured and rehabbing everyday but as basketball season approached, I found myself in the church gym alone beginning to jog and shoot some baskets.

I wasn't even a shadow of the player I used to be, but I was determined to be as good as I possibly could. I worked my rear end off all winter. I went to a few games to support my teammates, but it was hard to watch them. I had never missed a basketball season since grade school, and it hurt.

As winter turned into spring, I still longed to be on a team, to experience the camaraderie found in a united effort, the pride of representing your school, the discomfort of being packed shoulder-to-shoulder with other smelly boys on long bus rides.

My balance was improving, but I still hadn't gained enough stamina to conquer heavy physical activity with my mangled leg.

But that didn't stop me from trying out for my first varsity sport. Hello, Golf Team. Meet Chad.

I have to be honest here. I really wasn't pumped about golf as a sport. I didn't aspire to become a great player and help Lumberton High win the conference championship.

No. I just wanted to play a varsity sport. I wanted that varsity letter. And it didn't hurt that the golf team got to leave school at lunchtime on match days to play on some of the lushest courses in the Sandhills of North Carolina.

But even golf—with no running, no defense and no contact—wasn't easy. My Dad is a scratch golfer and coached the golf team at my high school many years before my time there. He was a huge help to me, but I was a football star and basketball player, so the finesse of the sport was lost on me. I was only trying to hit the ball as far down the fairway as possible. Grip it and rip it, John Daly style. This was not a great way to approach the game, but that was me. I could hit it far, but more times than not, it was far right!

A decade before pro golfer Casey Martin argued before the Supreme Court for the right to ride in a golf cart in PGA events, I was riding carts from hole to hole for the Lumberton High School golf team.

Because I was riding in a golf cart while the rest of my foursome walked the fairways, I missed out on a lot of the camaraderie that's shared on the course. My teammates were very supportive. It's just that their DNA was completely different than other teammates I'd had in other sports. Some were extremely focused, but not with the unleash-the-caged-beast intensity that permeates a football locker room. Instead it was a sophisticated, measured intensity that requires absolute mental concentration.

Golf, for me, turned into a lonely sport. No slapping each other on the helmet in the huddle between plays. No timeouts to gather at the bench and hear a coach yell "Who on this team has the guts to stand in front of No. 54 and deny him the ball?"

Hit a ball. Get in the cart. Drive to the ball. Hit it again.

No cheerleaders in short skirts on the fairways. No pep squad to decorate your locker with the school colors. Not even a crowd of over-involved parents to cheer when you dropped a 9-iron on the back of the green and drew it back toward the flag like it was magnetized.

Which didn't happen all that often for me, despite a competitive streak that was much stronger than my patchwork leg.

Did I mention that there were no cheerleaders in short skirts?

I had progressed a lot in walking with my prosthesis. But golf requires precision, and a wobbly stance will push a 300-yard tee shot

50 yards into the woods. And I could hit the ball farther into the woods than anybody on my team.

At the time, my Seattle foot prosthesis was state of the art. I also wore an orthotic on my right foot, which kept my ankle at a 90-degree angle. This kept me from dragging my toe when I walked over uneven ground. But it limited my flexibility, which affected my balance, especially on the rolling hills of a golf course. I had one leg that couldn't feel the ground, and the other didn't have the flexibility to help me hold my balance.

Even walking from the cart to my shot and back was a form of conditioning for my battered leg. But it was also enough to cause aggravating boils on my leg.

I was uncomfortable, but given the dramatic increase in my pain threshold the previous nine months, some raw skin didn't seem like an insurmountable challenge.

My scores weren't great, but I had enough raw athletic ability that I was able to crack the top six on the Lumberton High School team. That meant that my score could count in our matches. And it guaranteed that I would receive that coveted letter jacket.

The Spring Sports Banquet was a pretty special time for me. Normally, I don't make a big deal of recognitions and awards, but when I walked up to receive that big maroon and gold block letter "L" for my wool letterman's jacket, I was proud. I had been an all-star player, had been team captain and even MVP. But for me, that varsity letter trumped them all. I would rather have earned it for catching touchdown passes on the football team or grabbing rebounds on the basketball court, but this was my current situation, and I had overcome this obstacle—I was an athlete again!

Sometimes in life we get frustrated when we don't get what we want when we want it. Often the process is filled with bumps and hurdles and roadblocks. We want to change our goals or give up. We all want the end result. The riches. The fame. The successful business. Becoming a professional athlete, actor or musician. These are great aspirations, and you should always dream big. But nobody achieves lofty goals without many failures. Successful people also celebrate little victories along the way. Be proud of the steps that get you there. Don't rest in complacency but understand that the little steps will take you where you want to go. There is no express lane to success; you have to be patient and persistent.

Back on the Water

As the school year ended, the days lengthened, and the Carolina heat returned. Normally, we were all giddy with anticipation of another summer on the lake. The swimming, the boating, the girls . . . what's not to love?

However, the approach of the summer of '92 felt different for me and the rest of the Porters. Could I enjoy time at the lake while my buddies were out skiing and swimming? Would the sound of a boat engine rev up nightmares that I could never escape? Would all those girls in bikinis still admire my astonishing good looks? *Joking...*

The only way to find out was to load up the wagon and head to White Lake, our annual summer ritual. And this year, Mac and the Porters would arrive in style, towing a brand-new Ski Nautique. This was the Corvette of boats, and if you were anybody on White Lake, you had a Nautique.

The salaries of two hard-working educators in North Carolina don't result in copious amounts of extra income. But Mac and Pam always pulled together what they could to give Elise and myself great opportunities, including a boat to enjoy. I started out as a new skier behind a small outboard, moving up to an inboard/outboard

Glastron, and then the sweet Mustang 17. For my family, it was a really cool boat. It had tremendous power and sounded a little like a Harley Davidson on the water. The boat wasn't a frivolous expense, but an investment in memories and quality of life that our entire family will forever cherish.

We were satisfied with our Mustang and could have used it for years to come. But Correct Craft, the manufacturer of the Ski Nautique, learned about my accident. A representative from the company called my parents and told them to pick out a brand new Nautique, any color we wanted, and they would give us an extreme discount. It was the only way we were going to afford such an amazing boat. That summer, we arrived at White Lake to *oohs and ahhs* from our friends. More than 25 years later, that boat still runs as smooth as it ever did. We appreciated what we had and treated material things with care.

Having a new boat, of course, meant that I would be getting back on the water. I felt an internal pressure to face that challenge, even though no one was pushing me, I believe my parents wanted strongly to know that I wasn't scared to get back in a boat. Lake life was important to our family, and they prayed that my accident didn't take that from me.

Elise and my parents continuously encouraged me to take a spin. I had always believed that the previous year's accident was nothing more than a fluke, so I figured I would have no reservations about getting on the new boat. But it wasn't as easy as I thought. The first day we put the boat on the water my parents wanted me to get in the driver's seat and take it for a spin. When it was time to go, though, I hesitated.

The macho teenage boy in me said I wasn't scared. But for whatever reason, I wasn't ready. I had to prove to them I wasn't scared. And maybe, just maybe, to myself as well. When I fired up the engine and cruised away from the dock, I felt the familiar breeze, smelled the water and sunscreen and heard the sweet purr of a brand-new engine. I hit the throttle, and we sped across the lake like we were cutting glass.

I enjoyed driving the boat while my friends skied. I was still part of the group, and I got to be part of their enjoyment and exhilaration. But within a week or so, I grew restless. I wanted to ski!

I wasn't afraid for my safety, but I was super nervous about failing. I'm a very competitive athlete, and I had gotten really good at barefoot skiing, trick skiing and slalom skiing. I was not looking forward to starting over at the most basic level of water skiing while all my friends were advancing their skills and learning new tricks.

But I had no choice. I was going to have to swallow my pride and start with two skis. This was like going back to training wheels after riding off-road motorcycles. Sure, I occasionally skied on two skis, but only when jumping the floating ramp or when the Ski Heels were doing stunts like the pyramids. In my mind, I fought the notion that maybe I wouldn't even be able to balance myself, regardless of how wide the skis were or how calm the water was.

I was scared to fail.

I made my debut under my dad's watchful eye. Just getting the skis on became an ordeal. First, I put the wooden Alfredo Mendoza skis on the pier and lubed the rubber boots with liquid soap so that the immovable rubber prosthetic foot could be wedged tightly in the bindings. I slipped in my right foot next. The ski felt as heavy as a four-by-four block of lumber because of my limited strength and movement. The essential motion of dorsiflexion (flexing my foot up toward my shin) would be absent with all the permanent damage to the nerves in the lower leg. But I wasn't looking for excuses; I was preparing myself to succeed.

The water was still cool, and my heart was racing. I couldn't tell you if it was the temperature of the water or my nerves running wild in anticipation, but I had those internal shakes that would occasionally give you outward shivers. My dad threw me the rope handle, and the boat tightened up the slack.

I found myself back in grade school, remembering the most basic rules of skiing. Arms straightened. Knees bent. That beautiful new ski boat roared and pulled me up effortlessly. I wasn't quite as goofy as a newborn giraffe taking his first steps, but the struggle was real. Just like walking and golfing and a hundred other things I had to relearn—the more I worked at it, the more fluid my mechanics became. I was skiing almost a year to the day that had attempted to stop me forever.

I had overcome the pain in my legs, the doubt in my head, and an eerie premonition from a caricature artist.

Yes, you read that right.

Premonition?

The day before that infamous accident, I was in Myrtle Beach visiting family. Before Mom took me back to the lake to get ready for the next day's ski show, we stopped at a mall. I accidentally made eye contact with a caricature artist, so I felt obligated to let him draw me. He asked me what I liked to do and my name. That was it.

With his "canvas" turned so I couldn't watch what he was drawing, he created his masterpiece. I was born with a large head, so the drawing was bound to be comical. As he finished with a smile, he turned the easel around to reveal a pretty neat drawing.

There I was with my extra-large bubble head being pulled by a ski boat and I was on two skis cutting through the water. Here is where it got a little creepy. Chasing me from behind was a huge-toothed shark, bearing down fast. No big deal! Kinda neat! He must have assumed I did most of my skiing on the ocean, but that was irrelevant. Just 24 hours before I lost my leg in a ski boat accident, the caricature artist had penned at the top of the drawing in bright red letters, *Chad's Last Ride.*

It still gives me chills today to think about it.

Imagine my mom returning home after weeks of being at the hospital, going into my abandoned bedroom and seeing that drawing on my dresser. Neither of us thought a thing about it at the time of its creation, but was it an ominous premonition?

While I was at Duke, Mom removed the drawing from my room and boxed it up. For years, I never thought about it. After everything turned out OK, she handed it to me. By then, we could laugh about it.

But I will add this. I have passed many caricature artists since then, and I will NEVER have another drawing done again! Thank goodness, he was wrong that day. It was not my last ride!

Summer

Having a "normal" summer was a refreshing change from all the drama and tragedy of the previous summer. For the Porter children, that meant that in addition to all the fun on the water, it was time to get a job. My parents didn't consider coddling me because of my circumstances. The last thing I needed was to be treated as anything but a normal teenage kid. I was expected to pull my weight around the house, and I was also expected to continue to do some sort of work. My sister was always helpful around the house and, as a teenager, she worked at some of the local establishments around the lake. I had made a little money as a youngster mowing lawns every summer. After all, I needed some cash to support my Dairy Queen Blizzard addiction and to hand to the carnies who convinced me that yes, I was absolutely man enough to take that baseball and knock over those canvas puppet heads. Looking back, I could have just had my clients directly deposit my mowing money to Goldston's arcade and ride complex, and I wasn't the only one.

Now that I was 16, I decided that I was tired of having a kid job, so I was determined to find a real job! I landed my first official job with a huge campground at the lake called Camp Clearwater, and my ego swelled with the idea of doing some worthwhile, important work. The Camp Clearwater boss placed me on the grounds maintenance crew, and before I knew what was happening—I found myself mowing grass all over again. But this time I was riding on a tractor, so I was certainly moving up in the world. My crew mowed and trimmed the entire campground from Monday till Friday, and we started the whole process over the next week.

That summer, I learned about the pros and cons of blue-collar work. I liked working outside, but in the heat of the Carolina summer, my residual limb would slide around inside the socket of the artificial limb. My stump sweated profusely, and there was no way for the moisture to be released or absorbed. I could feel the discomfort, but I refused to ask for special treatment. I simply ignored the heat and pain and sucked it up. I didn't want to appear weak in front of the other guys and have them think that I couldn't handle the workload. As I protected my pride, the pressure points on my stump led to boils that would get infected and swell. There is no relief inside those carbon-graphite wrapped sockets, and it was so painful to press all my weight against those tender spots with every step I took.

Finally, one boil got so painful that I asked a doctor to look at it. What a colossal mistake that was! The doctor examined the infected boil, pulled out a scalpel and slit it open to drain the pus. I was forced for about a week to be without my prosthetic leg, and it was awful. I was having flashbacks of the previous summer, but skin problems are commonplace for amputees. I have since learned not to go directly to the doctor when these issues arise, and I have learned to drain them myself through creative ways. Please don't take this as my advocating for you to do the same thing. And children, don't try this at home.

Summer would not be complete without my week at House Party. For some people, going to a family reunion can cause anxiety and near depression, but for us Porters, there is nothing we like better. We gather with close to 200 relatives for an entire week! Cousins travel from all over the US to gather at White Lake for fun in the sun. As a kid growing up, this was the highlight of our entire year. The House Party of '92 could not have come at a better time for me. The previous year, I had made an appearance, but I was bound to a wheelchair and wasn't allowed to get into the water. This time, I was fresh off my bedridden week, and I was ready to play and have some fun before the start of the new school year.

The end of summer is always marked with a tinge of nostalgic sadness, even more so for the families who summered at White Lake. But this summer's end was especially tough on me. I had experienced a lot of growth and had done my best to make up for all the fun I missed the year before. Inevitably, we had to leave our happy spot to head back to Lumberton and the grind.

The time had arrived to repack our life and reconnect with friends to discover what everyone else did during their break. As sad as I was to leave the lake, I was still excited to be headed back to Lumberton for a new school year, and I wasn't nearly as nervous about entering the school doors this year.

Chapter 7:
Back on the Court

Pirate Basketball

Over the past six months, I had grown stronger and gained stability. I managed to jog a little, and twist and turn, and jump. But I still wasn't the athlete I wanted to be.

Another football season started without me. It didn't seem to matter that the coach didn't pass me a jersey, that somebody else was taking my place in the huddle, or that my teammates didn't need me leaping into the air to catch passes between two linebackers.

My football fate had been decided the year before. My doctors highly advised against me playing football ever again. There are times when I wished I had not listened to them, but I took some solace in the fact that the doctors hadn't forbidden me from playing basketball.

Despite the heavy depression that had blanketed me when I first saw that video of amputees playing their version of basketball, I still loved the game. I still played in the backyard and I had worked my way back into pickup games with friends and recreational church leagues.

At this point, I wasn't as quick or as agile as I was before the accident, but I had regained some strength and I was still one of the tallest guys around.

As I played in these semi-organized games, I stopped being a cocky kid proving that he could still play. I became another guy on the court who set picks, who traded elbows and who grabbed a lot of rebounds. I had learned how to fall and how to get back up.

As a coach's son, I had instincts. I knew that you were going to spin back to your right before you even made that fake to the left. And I knew the game. I knew every person's role on the court, how every player had a purpose in each play and how sometimes that role was to clean up the mess if everything fell apart.

But a few minutes of church league ball wasn't North Carolina High School basketball. Inspiration was all around us. We didn't have to travel far to see college superstars at UNC, Duke, N.C. State, or Wake Forest. Christian Laettner was at Duke, Fire and Ice (Chris Corchiani and Rodney Monroe) had just left N.C. State and Eric Montross was arriving on the scene for the Tar Heels.

My father had been a high school basketball coach, and I never missed one of his games. I idolized those Lumberton High School players—in my eyes growing up, they were the best around. They were cool and confident, and they instilled pride in the community.

Being a Pirate was a big deal. We were one of the largest schools in the state, and we played in one of the best conferences. If you were one of the twelve good enough to wear that jersey, you had reason to be proud. You wore your jersey to school on game days, and you felt like you were part of something important, something special.

So that fall when I showed up for basketball tryouts, I'm sure there were plenty of skeptics. I would have to prove myself like every other player on the court. There were no provisions in the rulebook for a player with a prosthesis. So, if I was slower than everyone else or couldn't jump as high, it didn't matter that I only had one good leg.

Basketball tryouts at Lumberton High School were a survival of the fittest. The coach's goal, it seemed, was to make the practices so physically challenging that players would give up and not come back.

I had never been the type of player to let hard work keep me from achieving anything. But I also had never tried to play high school basketball with one leg. There wasn't anyone doing what I was attempting to do at that level, and I was excited that I might be the one to break the barrier. I was excited to be one of the first to ever play highly competitive sports with an artificial limb.

Conditioning was brutal. When I walked off the court the first day, I thought I was going to die. Each practice took a devastating toll on my body. And even my psyche was challenged during the "boot camp" style practices. For days and days, I told myself, "I'm never going to be able to do this." But in the same breath I was determined to give it everything I could.

Sweat caused my leg to slide around in my prosthesis. I was rubbing blisters on my leg from the shearing. I hadn't yet regained my wind, and my muscles were still in rebuilding mode.

I had to expend twice as much energy as someone with two good legs. But I endured the pain. I got no special treatment. When the team ran suicides at the end of a three-hour practice, I ran suicides. When the team practiced defensive slides until their thighs burned with pain, I kept practicing defensive slides right alongside them.

As the weeklong tryout process neared an end, my body was spent. My right leg ached incessantly, my prosthetic connection was rubbed raw and my body hurt all over.

But I kept pushing with every scrap of energy I could muster. It would have been so easy to just walk away and take credit for an inspiring effort. But I needed to prove to myself that even the most impossible situations can be overcome. At the last tryout practice, I was heaving and panting and grinding to keep up with the rest of the players. I wondered how long somebody could keep pushing their body to its absolute limit. But I didn't dare stop. I had to make the roster. I had set a goal and had announced it by showing up at tryouts. My parents knew, my friends knew, and everyone associated with Lumberton High School sports knew.

I couldn't fail in front of all of them. Mostly, though, I had to prove to myself that these legs would not prevent me from achieving something I desired so much. I just had to succeed.

As long as I could stand, I could run. It was just a matter of mental toughness to make myself keep moving forward on the last day of tryouts. I was surviving, but just barely.

As I powered my way through a drill early in practice, the coach came over to me.

Did he think I was dogging it? Did he think I couldn't handle the rigors of a full basketball season?

I braced myself for disappointment.

"You're on the team, Porter," he said. "Take it easy today."

I will cherish that moment forever. All the pressure that I'd loaded on myself was suddenly lifted.

I no longer had to prove myself. I was no longer confined by these battered legs. I had worked harder for this than anything else in my life, and I had succeeded.

I could compete for the high school team. I could wear the school colors with pride. Parents would come to watch. And the cheerleaders in those short skirts . . . well, they'd be cheering for me.

Once I made the team, in my mind, at least, the story shifted. Though the pain persisted, the anxiety subsided. This was no longer about whether the amputee could make the team. Now I wanted to become the best player I possibly could be.

For a lot of people, just trying would have been enough. Maybe they would have been satisfied to play at the most basic level of those men in the video I saw in my hospital room. But to me, that meant nothing. I told myself repeatedly, "You're going to be the absolute best you can be, or you're not going to play."

Despite all of my work and determination, my conditioning had not overcome all those months of inactivity. Still, I had all the confidence in the world that as long as my leg didn't fall off, I could be one of the best players on the team. I could guarantee one thing, no one was going to work harder than I was. My work ethic had been ingrained in me from my parents—from my Dad on the courts and fields, and by my mom in the classroom. Of all the parents who ever parked their fannies on a wooden bleacher, Mac and Pam were the best.

My dad had spent thousands of hours working with me on my basketball skills at home. My home court was a circular patio. The goal was mounted on a painted plywood backboard mounted to an iron frame with U-shape brackets we attached around a metal pole we set in the ground.

I was very lucky to have a Dad who could make things and fix almost anything. The basketball goal was one of many do-it-yourself projects my dad let me help with, and it provided everything I needed to enjoy the game. Dad stressed the importance of having good form when learning to shoot the ball, so the goal was designed to be raised as I grew older and got stronger. Of course, my friends and I occasionally lowered it, so we could imitate the dunks we saw on *SportsCenter*.

Dad installed a spotlight over the court, and there were many weekend nights when I would practice my free throws and count down the last few seconds of an imaginary championship game in my PJ's until 11 o'clock. My parents would drag me inside, and my only solace was that as soon as the sun rose, I could come back out and play some more.

I never played to please my parents. I played because my dad instilled in me a love for the game. Dad and I bonded under that basketball goal, where he taught me the jump hook. "If you can master this shot," he said. "Nobody can stop you." I was constantly working on my footwork and balance. Until I was proficient with my left hand, he refused to let me dribble with my right. Throughout my youth, he inspired me to become the best player I could be. And though I didn't really consider it when I returned to the court as a teenager, I was about to inspire a lot of people myself.

As the first game approached, I got butterflies in my stomach. But they didn't originate from doubt. No, these were familiar butterflies of excitement—the same ones I experienced every time I put on a uniform to represent my school.

I was ready to play.

The Cover-Up

When I think back to childhood, so many of my happiest memories revolve around sports. When our phones had spiraling cords and not megapixel cameras, Dutch Huebner and I used an old-school Polaroid to try to capture our dunks on actual film. We launched ourselves off a patio chair and imagined ourselves dunking over some giant NBA center in a photo that would appear on the cover of *Sports Illustrated*.

I absolutely loved playing sports, and they helped define who I was. After my injury, my dreams of college scholarships were virtually shattered. But my love for the game had not been diminished.

My goals for Lumberton High School were to play to the best of my ability, and to do so with no special provisions.

I feared that if my opponents saw my artificial leg, they wouldn't compete as hard against me. I would be the one-legged guy. If you found yourself playing pick-up ball on some random basketball court and you were chosen to guard a one-legged man, are you going to guard him as hard? Are you going to push him around like everyone else? Probably not.

And I refused to let it happen that way.

I wore knee-high socks to conceal my prosthesis, which was shaped exactly like my other leg. The socks also concealed the foot brace and the scars on my right leg. I wore a knee brace to support the prosthesis connection just below my left knee. When I was fully dressed, I stood out like Kurt Rambis on those great Laker teams. No one in the early 90's was wearing high socks anymore. This was the era of ankle socks below the shoe line. I was no fashion trendsetter, but I was on the court to play.

To opponents, cheerleaders and fans in our opponents' gyms, I just looked like the white kid with the goofy knee-high socks. If you didn't know my story, you would never have guessed that I had lost a leg. And that's exactly what I wanted. With socks covering all evidence of the accident, you couldn't see that anything was wrong.

I don't recall my first appearance as a monumental event. I was on the team and we played basketball, just as we had in eighth and ninth grades.

There may have been a few more fans at the Lumberton High School games to see the one-legged guy play. And there was probably some pointing and whispering in the stands from those who knew my story. But I was oblivious to anything happening off the hardwood. I was boxing out, rebounding and defending the post.

My plan to keep my opponents from knowing about my situation worked. I would bang against them for four quarters, trading elbows and outworking them to gather loose balls. I gave them my best effort, and I got theirs in return.

Sometimes, after the game, my coach would pull me out of the locker room.

"Chad, somebody wants to talk to you," he would say.

Sometimes, the opposing coach would shake my hand, applaud my tenacity and flatter me with words about courage and inspiration. Other times, the opposing coach would ask me to visit his locker room. And the coach would make a speech about hard work and courage and he'd ask me to show them my legs.

When I rolled down my socks, their jaws would drop at the sight of a hairless, rubber leg and the other covered in gruesome scars. Most of them had never seen an artificial leg, and they couldn't have imagined that they were playing against a guy who had one. I remember one instance where the coach for South View High School called me into their locker room. There I had the opportunity to show off in front of one of the best high school players I've seen play in person, Jeff Capel. He was a beast in high school and was destined for Duke, where he scored 14 points in the National Championship game his freshman year. After his amazing career at Duke, he became head coach at Virginia Commonwealth, Oklahoma, then associate head coach at Duke, and then Head Coach at Pittsburgh. When I played against him, he was just an amazingly talented teenager, and he acted humbled to meet me! This was my first glimpse that I might have something special going on.

"Unbreakable"

Playing high school basketball soon became routine for me. I clicked my leg into place, dressed it up and I played as hard as I could. I wore the Flex Foot, one of the first prostheses designed specifically for athletes. It was a huge upgrade from the Seattle Foot that I was given initially. The spring and the bounce enhanced my gait and athleticism more than words can describe. My speed increased. My jumping was back to pre-injury height. I played with reckless abandon, running and jumping with all the force I could muster.

We were enjoying a solid season when we came to Southern Pines to play Pine Crest High School. The gym was packed with basketball fans, the pep band filled the arena with sound, and the smell of popcorn fueled the fun, as the game tipped off. For the first time, my prosthetist Danny Ellis, who had helped me fit my new leg, was going to see me play. He sat beside my parents in the stands as they all watched in nervous anticipation with the other parents.

The game was competitive, and I was working hard to help us battle one of our rivals. In the first half, I jumped high to grab a rebound. Without thinking I turned to my left, where I knew our guard would be awaiting the outlet pass. I flung the pass up court, and as our offense moved into fast-break attack mode, I fell down. Falling was a skill I perfected after the accident, but I was equally adept at getting up.

As my teammates were pushing the fast break, I scrambled to my feet. Just as I planted, my left leg buckled, and I went down again. There was no pain, I couldn't understand what had happened. Then I discovered the problem. My leg—the indestructible prosthesis—was snapped in two. It was still covered by foam and rubber skin, but the metal "bones" inside had broken completely in half.

Since the action had rushed to the other end of the court, hardly anybody had seen me fall. But once the basket was made, the referees stopped the game.

I was angry, knowing that I wouldn't be able to play the rest of the game. I had started hopping off the court on my right leg. No pain. No grimace. Just a mad young man hopping back to the bench. A collective gasp emanated from the crowd and I saw the shock and horror on the faces of the opposing team's fans. I was confused. What was so horrifying? A few teenage girls looked my way and literally ran screaming from the gym.

That's when it hit me. Those fans didn't know I had an artificial leg.

I looked down at my left leg. My foot and ankle dangled limply, rotating unnaturally in complete circles and swinging flimsily as I hopped. To someone who thought I had actual bones under my layers of socks and braces, it was a gruesome sight, ranking right up there with Joe Theismann's broken leg. Imagine had Paul George of USA Basketball gotten to his feet and hopped off the court after snapping his leg in two. That's exactly the visual this packed gym had, minus the blood.

My coach was in disbelief: "You gotta be kidding me!" was all he could muster.

My parents were devastated, my teammates laughed, and my prosthetist was bewildered.

Bless the hearts of the Pinecrest players because, as I hopped to the bench and as the crowd dry heaved, they tried to help as much as they could. In their minds, I had just brutally snapped my leg in two, and my teammates were not helping. In fact, they were laughing at the reactions. The opponents ran beside me begging me to lay down. "Just get on the floor, man!" They pleaded for me to stop moving. But they absolutely were not prepared or willing to touch the leg. All I could do at the moment was yell at them, "Get away from me, I'm FINE!" I still laugh when I think about their faces and their concern for me, and I wonder if they ever learned what really happened.

Over the next few years, we got to know my prosthetist very well. He was challenged year after year to fit me with an "unbreakable" leg, and every year I proved the prosthetic company's slogans wrong.

I have broken eleven "legs" altogether. When Danny attached a new state-of-the-art leg, he insisted that I test it before we left his office. One time I ran, I jumped, I landed hard, and it snapped before I even got to take it home. Can I tell you how freaky it is when the carbon graphite decides to explode? It sounds like a shotgun going off and you never know it's coming. Over time, I started collecting legs so that when the next one broke, I would have a spare to replace it.

At the end of the season, I was filled with a sense of accomplishment. Despite my occasional prosthetic problems, I had accomplished what many would never have attempted. I had become one of the first amputees in the country to play highly competitive sports with an artificial leg. I don't consider myself a trailblazer who started any kind of movement for amputees, but I do hope that I inspired some of those who crossed my path. I was beginning to see the impact that my life story could have on others.

When you are wrapped up with life, trying to survive, trying to be normal, fighting to fit in and become who you want to be, you don't think about inspiring people. Think of the people who inspire you. They didn't set out to inspire you; they set out to accomplish and overcome. Their inspiration is an organic result of their genuine dedication, perseverance, character and success.

I've never been motivated by someone seeking attention for being something they are not. I gravitate toward the selfless, those who can inspire with their infectious spirit and determination. They don't feel the need to tell everyone how awesome they are. They live their lives as an example and expect absolutely nothing in return. No one cares what you know until they know how much you care.

When you see a purpose brewing for your life, it's an exciting time. I was just beginning to understand that maybe there was something special about my story. Still, I was too young and distracted to fully realize the extraordinary circumstances behind my situation. Playing high school basketball was a significant achievement, and one that many doubted would happen after my accident. My story was still unfolding, though. I still had a lot to experience and much more to learn.

I wasn't consciously planning how I could be an inspiration or what my next big obstacle I could accomplish. I was a teenager living my life and trying to figure out who I was. But I knew that I was different. I knew that I stood out. Time would tell whether I would stand out for the right or wrong reasons. We all are impactful on others as we go through our lives. We will discuss impact later in the book, but as we continue our journey, start to examine your life and how you are and could be impactful for others.

Chapter 8:
Regaining Confidence

Summer Fun

The summer before my senior year, I started to feel more like the kid who put on that gorilla suit at Tucker Lake two years earlier. I had been forced to mature faster than I wanted to, but I was still that daring, fun-loving teenager.

I was looking forward to a summer without major physical obstacles. Long days working in the heat of the sun capped off with nights of cruising the lake with friends. Moonlit nights on the dark waters, night swimming, and serenading cute girls with the acoustic sounds played by Lee Hauser's guitar and the "melodic" voices of post pubescent boys who truly believed they sounded just like Boyz 2 Men. We were either pretty darn good at harmonizing or there were a lot of tone-deaf teenage girls. Either way, we had a blast.

On the occasional Friday and Saturday night, we would load into someone's car and head to Myrtle Beach. It's the land of neon, putt-putt golf, all-you-can-eat seafood buffets and thousands of teenage girls in bikinis. Sometimes, we would head to a nightclub where me and my crew of water-skiing buddies danced in the cages till 2 a.m.

I could keep up with them on the dance floor, and before long, I was catching back up to them on the water. The slalom, kneeboard, and wakeboard were all conquered during that first summer. The more runs I attempted, the more my confidence grew.

Once I discovered that there was no way to really hurt myself any more than normal, the crazy "I'll try anything" Chad was back for good. I am convinced that you have to be a little crazy and fearless to ever be great at something. Talent and dedication can help you achieve some success, but until you get completely out of your comfort zone, you will never realize your true potential. This is the absolute truth when it comes to any physical accomplishment, and waterskiing specifically. You gotta have guts to try new things and push your body. I never lacked courage, and as my "good" leg strengthened, I regained my confidence. I was getting pretty good on the water once again.

That's not to say that there weren't a few blunders along the way. Fortunately, I have always been able to laugh at myself.

One gorgeous Saturday when the weekend warriors were all squeezed onto the lake like pepperonis on a pizza, the crew and I decided to head out to do a ski session and see who we could impress. Except for early mornings and late evenings, we didn't normally ski on weekends during the summer due to the rough water churned up by the influx of boats. On this day, the boat was packed with friends, all rooting each other on. When my turn arrived, I wanted to work on a couple of flips on the wakeboard. With the boat zipping along on the water, I leaned hard on a cut outside the wake in order to have plenty of room to pick up speed heading back to hit the wake for lift-off. Coming in perfectly, I launched into the air and began the rotation. I could tell that I had caught some air and I knew I was looking good!

Until it was time to land. Apparently, I had admired my lift a little too much. It felt so good to be upside down in the air that I forgot to continue my rotation. The nose of my board caught the water, and I was body slammed into the lake. Water can be very soft and relaxing when you knife through it like a diver, but it can also feel like pure concrete when you crash into it unexpectedly.

I slammed into the lake with so much impact that my right foot slipped right out of the wakeboard boot. My left prosthetic foot, which requires dishwashing soap as a lubricant in order to release, didn't budge. Something had to give, though, and the weak spot was the joint between my nub and the prosthetic leg. I shot out of the leg like a cannon and found myself floundering to find the surface. I was scared that my prosthetic leg would sink to the bottom of the lake!

Once I surfaced, my worry was overtaken by amazement. I had been dumped into the lake, but my prosthetic leg, designed to look like a real leg, was still scooting across the lake on the wakeboard. It looked as if the half leg was on a run of its own.

Soon, it caught the attention of the other boaters, and they justifiably freaked out! Boats and jet skis were about to run into each other as people pointed and screamed. Even in my own boat, people were losing their minds. I remember poor Daryl Smith, who had been at Tucker Lake the day of my accident, couldn't do anything but cover his face. Afraid that I would somehow hurt myself, he wouldn't even watch my runs. After that fiasco, I figured he would never get in a boat with me again. I have a feeling that there are a lot of people who will never forget the day they saw half of a leg wakeboarding across White Lake!

Senior Year

When my senior year of high school arrived, I had high hopes of a year filled with sports and fun and, of course, good grades. In addition to my annual goals, I set my sights even higher for my senior year—I decided to run for Student Body President. I was involved with student government throughout my school years, so leading my classmates during our final year could be the culmination of my efforts.

The superficial part of campaigning, making silly posters and handing out candy or trinkets, did not appeal to me at all. But I was looking forward to getting on stage and debating about why I was the best candidate. I truly believed I would do a fantastic job helping to be a voice for my classmates. I ran against Candace Wooten, who was way smarter than I was. She was a borderline genius and defeating her wasn't going to be easy.

The race was decided by the final few votes, and somehow, I squeaked out a win. I was excited that my fellow students had recognized my sincerity and chosen me to represent them.

But the exhilaration of achieving a monumental goal was stifled by the words I overheard just moments after my victory had been announced on the school intercom. And I remember them as if they were said to me yesterday.

"I'm sure they just voted him to be President because they felt sorry for him."

Kids can say some dumb and hurtful things sometimes, can't they? That kind of put-down was nothing I hadn't already dealt with over the past two years. I should just ignore the comments and feel good about my accomplishments because you can't control what comes out of a high school kid's mouth, right? Well, that's exactly how I would have responded had it been a teenager who had said such a thing. Unfortunately, those ignorant, inconsiderate words spilled out of the mouth of a teacher just as I was walking past her and a colleague in the hallway.

Wow, did she really just say, what I thought she just said?

At that moment, I knew I had still more to prove to people. The teacher's comments confirmed my fears that others thought I was receiving special treatment, and it wasn't just my peers. I was always taught to respect my elders, but on that day, it became clear to me that adults aren't always right. Age, experience, and education do not automatically make you a more considerate person.

I will always respect my elders. But bullying and back-stabbing and being ugly isn't reserved for the young. It's everywhere. All ages. We are all flawed, and we all make mistakes, but the difference lies in our intentions.

Here's a pretty simple rule—Never say anything *about* somebody that you would not say *to* that person's face.

That should pretty much take care of most boneheaded, hurtful comments.

Whether you intend to hurt someone with your words doesn't matter. You never know who is listening to your jokes and jabs. Once those words pierce your lips, they can never be taken back. Your reputation is painted by your deeds and words. Don't be reckless and let offhand comments stain your character. Learn to use that filter you were given by God, your brain.

We must be aware of how dangerous our tongues can be. We may never know the scars they leave.

Note on the Windshield

I graduated from Lumberton High School shortly after my sister, Elise, graduated with her education degree from UNC Greensboro. As soon as I walked across that stage, my family and I boarded a cruise ship. My parents and grandparents had planned the cruise as a celebration of our achievements.

My grandparents were amazing people. Dad's parents and Mom's parents got along so well that they would often take vacations together. Dad's mom, Mema, was a tough woman and was forever proud that she taught for over 40 years and influenced practically every kid that came through the public-school system in Elizabethtown, NC. My mom's parents, Mary and Joseph (I kid you not) would take Elise, me and our cousins Seth and Sara Beth on some kind of adventure every summer. I always looked forward to these trips, packing in the back of that huge wood-paneled station wagon and heading to some resort location. Of course, I never realized how brave they were to travel for days with four young children! I can only hope I have acquired a fraction of their patience.

On the cruise, we enjoyed a week of sun, sightseeing, and endless buffets. I was soaking up life and reflecting on how much had changed, and how much I had accomplished in the past two years.

When we returned home after the cruise, I found a note on the windshield of my Jeep. Kelvin, my best friend, wrote a short message for me to call him the second I returned. I had not had any contact with anyone from Lumberton in seven days, and this seemed like an ominous message.

I ran to the phone and called Kelvin. The second I heard his voice; I knew something terrible had happened. In a somber tone, he told me that our good friend Jimmy had died. I couldn't believe my ears. This can't be happening, I thought. Jimmy was the salt of the earth, a kid who never so much as breathed a bad word to anyone. He was a great-looking kid and an amazing athlete. We played high school basketball together and grew up in the church together.

Like the incident that nearly killed me, Jimmy's accident involved a boat. He was washing his boat in the stall of his family's dock on Lake Waccamaw when he backed up into a frayed wire. The jolt of electricity from the wire instantly electrocuted him.

I rushed over to Jimmy's house, where I was met with a huge gathering of friends consoling each other. After hugs from Kelvin and a few others, I found myself face to face with Jimmy's parents at the front door. His dad hugged my neck tight and said he had been waiting for me to get back from our trip. I didn't have any comforting words.

All these thoughts raced through my head. This is so unfair and so heartbreaking for this family. I wondered why I was spared that day of my accident. Why wasn't Jimmy? He deserved to live. He was a better kid than I was. I wished I had the right answers to tell his dad that night on the porch. Instead I just hugged him and loved him. It was all I could do.

Several of Jimmy's friends, including me, were asked to be pall-bearers for Jimmy's funeral. Throughout the service, I felt my own pain of losing such a good friend, but I couldn't imagine the pain his family must have been dealing with. Had things happened just a little differently at Tucker Lake, that could have been my family grieving the loss of their teenage son.

I realized during this time, and for weeks after, that sometimes life just sucks. There are no explanations for why things happen. I felt very lucky to be alive. I thought about what my parents would be going through had I not survived my experience. It's hard to swallow sometimes.

Jimmy's death was my first real experience losing someone close to me and someone so young. I don't think it ever gets easier. I have gone through waves of emotions over the years dealing with death and loss, and I have learned there is no right or wrong way to get through those times. You can't judge your actions or reactions as wrong or right, or try to compare yourself with how others are coping. Some cry, some make jokes to distract themselves, some shut down, and some seem to be in total control. We all process them in our own way.

The last time I saw Jimmy on this earth, I had no idea I would never speak to him again. But he knew I had the utmost respect for him. I plan to see Jimmy again someday, and I hope he is proud of me.

Chapter 9:
College Life

Career Inspiration

I visited quite a few universities across North Carolina, but I was destined for the University of North Carolina at Wilmington! The gorgeous campus was minutes away from Wrightsville Beach. Fortunately, UNCW also offered a major that would correspond to my life's ambition.

I was convinced beyond a shadow of a doubt that I wanted to become a Physical Therapist. Even though my entire family was in education, I didn't feel drawn to that field. PT's help people every day, and they make good money. My involvement in sports and the extensive therapy I had endured made me an ideal candidate for the PT program. I had everything planned out in infinite detail. I would need to get my undergraduate degree and complete my prerequisites to apply for Physical Therapy School. All programs at that time were master's level, so I would need to attend graduate school as well. Next to being a professional athlete, this was the best fit for me. I was excited about my future.

College didn't disappoint me for one instant. Lumberton was only about 90 minutes from campus, and I remember thinking that I would come home most weekends and see the family and my high school buddies. *Ummm . . . no!* Instead, I quickly made new friends, fell in love with UNCW and Wilmington and rarely made it back to Lumberton.

College was an amazing time of independence, growth and learning from mistakes. My time was filled with friends, intramurals, volunteering, some beach time, and obviously tons of studying. The relationships that I developed there will always fill me with positive memories. From roommates to classmates to professors, I have maintained a core group that I feel at any time I could call on if I ever needed anything.

Look at Those Legs

I had come a long way physically and emotionally since my accident, but there were still lingering challenges that I hadn't completely overcome. I still felt more comfortable in long pants than I did in shorts.

I wish I could better explain why I felt the way I did. I think that the youth of today feel the same way about the seemingly insignificant hang-ups they are dealing with. As if their feelings aren't enough to share with others for help. The desire to be like everyone else and to blend in with the crowd is so powerful that the slightest notion that we are different in any way can be devastating. What a shame that we feel that way at times. And this doesn't just apply to teens but to adults as well. I was still battling with this deep inside me while my exterior appeared completely in control. When I wore shorts, it was on the basketball court with the fellas that I quickly bonded with. They eventually saw me as a good, competitive basketball player and nothing else.

I still donned the "real" looking leg on a daily basis as if I was somehow fooling the world. I developed a tight group of new friends who knew my story and never blinked when I had to adjust my leg. When I was out meeting new people, though, I tried to blend in and cover up. If having a prosthetic leg is the first thing people notice about you, they treat you differently. They either awkwardly avoid discussing it, or it becomes the first topic of conversation.

During my freshman year I was so clear about my life's calling and pursuit to be a physical therapist that I wanted to volunteer as much as possible in the healthcare field to gain experience. Plus, it would look good on a grad school application.

Volunteering meant performing any task the professionals needed help with, and that was fine with me. I was happy to be in a healing environment and learn more about my field. During my time cleaning workout equipment at a rehab facility, I made an immediate connection with a gentleman named Brad Hornick. He was a prosthetist who had his own practice, and he was very interested in making me a new leg . . . for FREE! I know when something seems too good to be true that it usually is, so I tried not to let my hopes get too high. As I spent more time at Brad's office watching how his employees made limbs, I was extremely interested in seeing what he had in mind. Prosthetic legs cost thousands of dollars and have to be replaced every few years, so getting a brand new one would be a huge help to me and my family.

I assumed that Brad's team would recreate a realistic, lifelike leg similar to what I had grown accustomed to over the past several years. But Brad had his own plan. He quickly let me know that if he was going to build my leg, he was going to do it his way, and I was going to wear it. I agreed to wear whatever he made.

What I didn't know was that Brad's plan was not only to change the way my leg felt but to change the way I felt about my leg.

When I went in to try on the leg, he brought out a carbon graphite Flex Foot. The bolts and stainless steel were exposed for the world to see. But those things paled in comparison to the socket my leg would slide into. It was adorned with psychedelic colors and patterns that would make the late Jerry Garcia blush. If a satellite had passed over North Carolina, the leg would have been visible from the exosphere.

When I first saw the leg, I laughed. I didn't want to seem ungrateful, but . . . *You have got to be kidding me, right? You cannot expect me to wear this!* He was serious. Not only did this leg not resemble a real leg but you could see all of the machinery. I was being forced to make my leg a walking billboard announcing to the world "Hey look at me, I am an amputee." This went against every fiber of my existence since the accident. I had made it my life's work to minimize the attention brought to my leg; I just wanted to fit in with everyone else.

Brad said, "Once you go natural, you never go back." He said it in a lighthearted manner, but there was depth behind his words. Once you stop hiding behind the fake skin and shell, you will embrace who you are and love showing the world the mechanical leg and its components. I was not convinced at all, but I am a man of my word and I was gonna wear this wild appendage. *Time to suck up your pride, Chad, and be a man.*

The first time I walked through the mall, I immediately noticed a difference in the reactions of strangers. People did take immediate notice, but I didn't get the glaring stares and long investigative looks that I was accustomed to. Before, I had convinced myself that I was blending in with my skin colored leg, but I wasn't really fooling anyone but myself. People could tell there was something unnatural about my walk, but they couldn't immediately figure out what it was. People would stare as they tried to figure out what was wrong or different about my legs. I could see the looks and confusion, and I felt like I needed to explain myself. My new colorful addition, however, wasn't perplexing anyone. Most strangers gave a quick glance and responded with a smile. Some would say "Hey buddy, awesome leg!" What a crazy experience this was becoming! The positivity that was coming from this was encouraging, and I was actually starting to embrace being different.

Brad had known all along that converting me to the "natural" look would completely change my perspective. I couldn't believe it. His experience in the field and his belief in me helped me grow into a more confident young man. Even though I resisted initially, I could never thank him enough. I am convinced that God puts people in our lives that can help make a difference. We just have to be open to accept them and their goodness.

Confidence in who you are and who you have been designed to be is a game changer. It rarely comes easy, and for many, it never comes. We are specifically formed in the eyes of our Creator who makes no mistakes. At times it feels like a curse to be different and stand out for whatever reason. Every one of us has been given a different fingerprint, different looks, different shapes and sizes, different talents, different personalities, different abilities, and different circumstances in life. I am not a mistake. You are not a mistake. We are perfectly made. This world would be a terribly boring place if we were all the same. Once you embrace your uniqueness, you can enjoy absolute freedom. Start appreciating all the amazing things about you! I know we have all heard this before, but I will repeat it because I lived it.

When I got my natural leg, I started to feel, not only comfortable, but proud of who I was. I immediately felt like an inspiration to people without even having to open my mouth. How powerful is that?

Love yourself. You deserve to be happy, and loving who you are unconditionally is where happiness begins.

Post College

As graduation neared, I applied to four Physical Therapy schools for my master's degree. With my good grades and volunteer experience, I figured I would be able to choose which grad school best met my needs. But when those envelopes arrived in the mail, they were filled with letters that said things like "We receive many applications . . ." and "Thank you for applying . . ."

I became quite humbled when I was not accepted into any of the four schools I applied to. This eventually became another "meant to be" moment for me as I was forced to work for another year until I could reapply. Delaying my education certainly was not in MY plan, but it was out of my control. Becoming a PT was still my destiny, so I decided to get a job where I could continue to learn and improve my application status. A year working as a PT Tech at the local hospital was exactly what I needed. Real-life, hands-on experience magnified all the knowledge I had learned in the classroom.

The lead therapist quickly realized that I could do more than clean equipment. By employing my experience and my skills to encourage and motivate our patients, the team realized that I could be a huge asset. The experience helped me land a spot in the best PT program in the state. I received early admission the following year to East Carolina University. I remember how excited I was when the letter came in the mail and it started with "Congratulations!" When I shared the good news with my friends, they took me out on the town to celebrate. I had no clue how amazing that night was about to become. It turned out to be a night that would change my life forever!

Stories that include a life-changing event after a night of drinking with friends generally do not end well, but in my case, that night was amazing. I saw this vibrant, beautiful girl. The rest of the room turned into a gray blur in comparison as I watched her from across the room. By some act of fate, she ended up chatting with my friends and me. When she found out why we were celebrating, she bought me a drink. I know people always envision meeting the love of their lives in a more romantic setting, but for my wife Desiree and me, our story started this incredible night. We danced all night. I couldn't stop staring and wondering why in the heck she wanted to hang out with me! We laughed as she sat on my lap at 2 a.m. devouring pizza at Vito's on Wrightsville Beach. I wanted to spend every second with her from that moment forward. We just clicked! Unfortunately, this would prove to be a tough time to start a relationship.

We would almost immediately have to endure a long-distance relationship as I went off to school, but her support for me was palpable.

We went through some ups and downs during this time, but we supported each other, and our relationship became stronger because of it. I remember many moments when I was so stressed because of the workload in PT School, especially in that first summer of Gross Anatomy, and the hours of phone calls to her in Wilmington that would bring me so much comfort. I was homesick from her often. She knew and felt it as well, but she never burdened me with her sadness. Ahh, young love. More than once, she just showed up on at my apartment door in the late evening. After a full day at work, she drove the 2 ½ hours to Greenville, just so we could spend a couple hours together before she had to drive back to Wilmington. She showed me then that she was willing to make sacrifices for us, and I came to appreciate what a considerate soul she is. She was by my side during grad school, and has always been supportive of my journeys and aspirations.

After two years of PT school, I returned to Wilmington and the rehab hospital where I had previously worked as a tech, just as I had planned. I loved working with my patients and seeing them progress. On my floor, we treated patients recovering from stroke, traumatic brain injuries, amputation and other complex diagnoses.

As I helped my patients make small incremental gains, I was reminded of my own tedious progress as I worked with Kathy during my after-school therapy sessions. And just as I celebrated overcoming milestones as a patient, I was gratified to be able to celebrate the milestones of my patients. Being a physical therapist can be tough at times, but it's so rewarding to help your patients do more than they thought was possible.

If you have ever worked in healthcare, you know that it's not often glorious or about saving lives. Every day, there are moments that test your patience. I was blessed to work closely with some incredible nurses, doctors, and therapists. We were divided into teams, and my partner in crime was an occupational therapist, named Mike Sblendorio. We helped a lot of people and had fun in the process.

One day Mike and I had a patient whose legs and pelvis had been destroyed in a vehicle accident. The patient was the father of a young boy, and his son's birthday was rapidly approaching. Despite his circumstances, the patient wanted to make sure his son received the perfect gift. I'm sure this was a very emotional time for him and the family, because he was unable to leave the hospital to buy a present. His wife came through, delivering the coolest remote-control monster truck we had ever seen!

Mike and I had the unique ability to relate to our patients no matter their medical situation, personality, or age. Like Dr. Harrelson at Duke, we were ourselves with everyone. We would have an elderly lady, in the direst of circumstances, singing to the top of her lungs as we walked her down the hallways. We cracked jokes with our patients to help brighten the atmosphere. So, it was no surprise that we decided to have a little extra fun with the monster truck.

We asked this super cool dad if we could borrow this awesome truck for a few minutes. He was all about helping us pull a little prank. We took a small plastic urine container, filled it to the brim with apple juice, and shook it up. The bubbles on the top were the perfect resemblance of what would normally fill said container. We then loaded up the back of the monster truck with an overfilled jug of "pee" and as we hid behind the med cart, we steered the truck down the hallway. Taped to the front of the truck was a note that read "Please empty me."

As the truck swerved, sped up and spun in a circle, the lid came loose, and the "juice" began to slosh out of the top. Nurses ran down the hall screaming, and patients were laughing hysterically. The fiasco went on for longer than it should, and no one could figure out how this truck was moving, but we all loved it! We finally cleaned up the truck like new and got a huge high-five from our favorite dad.

Workplaces can be stressful, and it's not always appropriate to cut up, but if you can't find some way to have fun and enjoy yourself while getting things done, you might need to find another place to work. Finding a way to bond with your coworkers, clients, patients, or visitors may be exactly what you need to keep your sanity and be a difference maker for those you come into contact with.

Because of my boyhood experiences, several friends told me, "I bet you can get your patients to do anything you want after you show them all you have been through." This could have been true, but I was very selective when deciding whether to reveal my story to my patients. Since my accident, I had learned that everyone's problems are different and the ways they cope with them also are unique. I remembered visitors who had come to my room to talk about how they had lost a limb or been through an accident that nearly claimed their lives. Some were very helpful, but some were a huge turn-off. Some people just comforted and encouraged without comparing their situation to mine, and I enjoyed meeting them and learning from them.

One person, however, visited me when I was in rehab learning to walk again. First, I want to say that I appreciate that he took his time to come by. He didn't leave me feeling any better, however. He was a cyclist who had lost his leg. As he spoke about his accomplishments, he was cocky and brash, and I knew he wasn't someone I wanted to emulate. I was at a point in my rehabilitation when I was trying to figure out what might be possible. Deep down, I was still hoping that I might be able to resurrect my football and basketball life. I remember the cyclist saying to me, "I doubt you will ever be able to play those sports again, but I can guarantee you that you can still ride a bike like me!"

While he meant his message to be inspirational, I only felt anger as he hobbled out the hospital door. I knew instantly that if I were ever in a position to speak to someone who had faced a tragedy, that I would never compare myself to them. If someone looks at me or hears my story and infers that if I can get through this, he can too, that's great. But those words will never come out of my mouth.

I did reveal my prosthetic and my story to a select few patients in an effort to gain their trust. I wanted them to know that I understood that what they were going through was hard, but I never said that I understood what they were feeling.

Our coping abilities and personalities develop over time and are not easy to change. Some patients feel like victims, and some see their injury or illness as their next challenge. I'm not here to say that one is right or wrong. You will never know what some people have seen and been through. Our individual experiences prepare us for life and how we deal with the tough times. Learning this valuable lesson helped me become a better healer, then as a physical therapist and later as just a listener.

I will never forget some of the most inspiring people I met during my time at the rehab, including patients and coworkers. A few of those individuals introduced me to a new outlet for my competitive side.

Chapter 10:
Wheelchair Basketball

Becoming a Spokesman

Tim Corbett, one of my rehab patients, was a United States veteran who had been paralyzed after flipping a Jeep while on duty. He was friends with Fred Smith, an above-the-knee amputee who lost his leg after it was crushed by a forklift.

When they heard that I was an athlete who had lost a limb, they asked me to play wheelchair basketball with their team, the Port City Spokesmen (great name, huh?). Even though I didn't use a wheelchair, as an amputee I was qualified to participate on the team. They asked again and again . . . repeatedly, and I declined politely.

I didn't see a reason to play in a wheelchair. I was still a great athlete playing basketball on my feet against some of the best players in Michael Jordan's hometown. Besides, I didn't need a wheelchair to do anything. It wouldn't be fair for me to play with these guys. I had fought so hard to get to the level of athletic ability of a great "able-bodied" person. Sitting in a wheelchair, in my mind, would be going in reverse. I was flattered, but it just wasn't for me.

But Tim and his teammates were as much salesmen as they were Spokesmen, and I eventually agreed to play; just for one practice, just so they'd have one more body to help fill the court. I have a sneaky suspicion they knew exactly what would happen in that practice at the YMCA.

Even though I no longer need a chair, I had gotten skilled at driving a wheelchair during my stint in rehab and occasional joy rides while I was working as a physical therapist. The Spokesmen provided a wheelchair to practice with, and in no time, I was maneuvering that chair like a dirt bike—holding wheelies for long rides down the court, turning 360s on a dime. Of course, I never doubted that I'd be able to shoot. My range was limited to about 15 feet with my mechanically sound shot, but I could hit longer shots by modifying my technique. A 10-foot goal looks far away from a seated position, but the rim and the backboard are just the same as they are in the city league games. My intent was to prove to them that I was far too good to be playing wheelchair basketball. This would probably be the last time they'd ask me to play.

Near the beginning of that first practice, I positioned myself near the basket. An errant shot bounced my way and I reached up and back to snag the rebound just as I had so many times for Lumberton High School and UNCW intramural teams. When I leaned back, though, my center of gravity shifted, and my wheelchair flipped backward, leaving me wallowing on the floor in a puddle of my own humility . . . and pain! *No problem. This was a fluke. I have this now.*

As my team moved down court to set up on offense, the other team's smallest player positioned his chair in front of mine and locked my wheel against his before I reached half-court. I pushed forward and backward and tried every maneuver I had to get around him. I busted my rear-end trying to just get down court and that little flea was having no part of it. By the time I made some progress, possession had shifted and the whoosh of wheelchairs had passed me going the opposite direction. *Wait, what?*

I wasn't used to being neutralized in a sporting event, so it was particularly humbling to be immobilized by the smallest player on the court.

Did I mention that I'm highly competitive? These wheelchair players were feeding me a huge slice of humble pie. After that first practice, my teammates gave me some advice on avoiding getting blocked out and other helpful strategies that were different from stand-up ball. And I went to another practice.

Pretty soon I had a jersey with my name on it, and I was traveling across the East Coast with these guys to play wheelchair basketball. The games are definitely more slugfest than hugfest. These men are die-hard competitors with no sympathy for anybody wearing a different-colored jersey. Discretely tipping over an opponent's wheelchair was a fairly common tactic used to gain an advantage. I saw more fistfights during wheelchair games than I ever saw during city league or intramural play. And more than once I saw players get knocked unconscious when a wheelchair flipped, and they hit the hardwood with their skulls.

But you can't underestimate the athletic ability of these players. Their bodies are different than traditional athletes, but they practice relentlessly to perfect the skills to succeed. They have as much heart, talent, drive, perseverance and grit as anyone I've ever played with or against. And they play with more passion and desire than those who coast on natural abilities and talents.

Every kid who participates in any sport should spend some time around the athletes that make up the Para-Sporting community. The kids should observe how hard these men and women work to pursue a passion and a love for their sport with an incomparable level of commitment. Kids too often are celebrated to such an extent that they believe they can excel on their talent and skills alone. So maybe if these young athletes could see wheelchair basketball players overcoming obstacles in everyday life and pushing themselves to excel, they might appreciate the value of dedication and hard work. Maybe they will realize that physical gifts and dogged determination can be a powerful combination.

Barrett's Story

One of my closest friends on the team, Barrett Allen, has one of the most powerful stories of overcoming life's obstacles, and I would be remiss if I didn't share a little of it with you.

Barrett is a true athlete. Always has been, always will be. As a quarterback for the Chugiak Mustangs, he was a record setter and the Alaska State Offensive Player of the Year!

After playing college ball for a couple of years he took off some time. He decided to return to college, and on the recruitment trip, his life forever changed. As he and a friend made a late trip back home, the driver fell asleep behind the wheel and they drove off the side of the Appalachian Mountains. For 10 hours their car laid against a tree fifty yards below the road with the roof crushed down on top of them. When they came to, Barrett was folded up at the waist with the tree trunk pressed down on top of him. He was unable to move from the pressure and the fact that his spine had been snapped. The driver laid with a mere scratch on his arm underneath the legs of my friend and struggled to free himself for hours. Finally, he was able to get back to the road to wave down help, but for Barrett, the damage was complete.

He would never walk again. He battled depression, drug abuse—both illegal and prescription. He struggled to find that identity that once gave him so much confidence. Years passed before he discovered wheelchair basketball. For an athlete like Barrett, rarely can anything fuel your passion and provide a sense of camaraderie like being a part of a team again.

Wheelchair basketball pulled him from some dark places and gave him a new outlook on life. He is amazing and is now married and helping to raise a son, all while working full-time as a counselor to people with disabilities and addictions.

Barrett inspired me to be a better player for my teammates and myself.

We all want the same things and finding an outlet to feel "normal" again is so important after a life-altering challenge.

Raising My Game

Not long after I started with the Spokesmen, we played in a huge tournament in Richmond, Va., against some formidable competition. I had improved tremendously in practices and had regained my confidence that I could dominate this sport.

But I was wrong. I was thoroughly embarrassed. It wasn't that I couldn't shoot and score, but I couldn't even get up and down the court to get into position, and constantly propelling the wheelchair was physically exhausting. My lungs weren't on fire like they would be in able-bodied basketball, but my arms were Jell-O. I pushed the wheels so hard to break past the defenses that my arms were completely limp when I finally got a chance to shoot. I had never struggled like this in a sport.

Many of my teammates lived their entire lives in chairs, and many didn't have the physical abilities I was blessed with. Trunk strength is massively advantageous in wheelchair sports, and some of our paralyzed players had no way to strengthen their cores.

I felt an obligation to have more of an impact on our success. I had to improve and quickly.

I worked hard at more skillfully controlling my chair. I noticed that many of the other amputees were strapped to their chairs. I wasn't, so I was constantly flopping around and falling out of my chair. Once I strapped myself to my chair, I became steadier, faster and more elusive. I could change direction and skirt around defenders without even touching my wheels. I quickly turned from being a hindrance on the court to an asset. Once my chair skills caught up with the shooting ability, I was able to help the Spokesmen win a lot of games.

And that sometimes made me a target for the opposing teams' fans.

Who's Booing Whom?

I found out that tournament spectators had little sympathy for a guy who didn't really need a wheelchair. During one game, my wheelchair sustained some damage that prevented me from moving and turning with any efficiency. At the next timeout, I wheeled over to the sideline, leapt out of my chair, attached my prosthesis and sprinted to the trailer outside to retrieve the toolkit so I could make repairs. As I rose from my chair, a chorus of boos rained down on me as if I had just knocked a baby out of its mother's arms.

They're booing me? I thought. *Didn't they hear about Tucker Lake? Don't they know how brave I am? Don't they understand what I've gone through?*

The gym was full of men who had lost the use of both legs during actual warfare. Some had debilitating diseases that left them with no use of their core muscles whatsoever.

And here I was—the guy who had lost half a leg in a boating accident. I wasn't going to get any sympathy.

My dad didn't understand why I would choose to sit in a chair when I could run and jump with some of the best players in Wilmington. And I'm not sure I could ever explain it to him, but there was inspiration to be gleaned from this experience.

Each road trip magnified my respect for these men. For me, a few hours of rigorous play in a manual wheelchair left my arms hanging from my body like wet noodles. My arms were so fatigued that my hands shook for days afterward when I picked up an ink pen.

Each day when the games were over, I hopped out of my chair and walked to the bathroom, to the car, to the hotel room. In contrast, my teammates, like most wheelchair basketball players, couldn't get anywhere without engaging their arms.

Each day when the games were over, my teammates would muster enough strength to transfer themselves into their everyday chairs, gather all of their equipment and gym bags, load them onto their playing chairs, and push both chairs out to their vehicles. At the car, they'd maneuver around the doors, load their basketball chairs onto the trailer and then lift their bodies into their cars. But that's not the end—then they would reach down and break down the everyday wheelchair, lifting the heavy metal frame and wheels over their bodies and into their car. Back at the hotel, they repeated the process in reverse to get back into their chairs and up to their rooms. At the hotel, they would use their arms to transfer in and out of shower chairs and eventually to their beds.

Even going to the bathroom is easier for me than for them. I could walk to the bathroom, unzip in front of the urinal and go. Some of my teammates had to roll through the bathroom door, insert a catheter and drain themselves.

I could not comprehend the hardships they endure every day to do every daily task that most of us never even think about. It's hard enough to live in a chair and handle all of life's physical barriers with just your upper body. So, how do these guys find the energy to bang around on the basketball court for hours, destroying their bodies?

Their grit and determination motivated me to work that much harder to improve, and I vowed that I would never again make excuses again for not being able to do something. I've seen enough people in far worse conditions accomplish the unthinkable. These athletes are the same as they have always been; they just have to work a lot harder to get to where they want to be.

As hard as they worked for everything in their lives, they deserved to experience some moments of athletic achievement. Together, we became a strong team, and we reached our loftiest goal—qualifying for the 2004 National Championships of Wheelchair Basketball.

Over 700 athletes traveled from all over the US and Canada to participate in championships in Illinois, and we played against some formidable competition, including teams sponsored by the

NBA. These were guys with biceps the size of my thighs wearing NBA replica uniforms—complete with warm-up outfits. This was a sharp contrast to our team, a bootstraps group that raised money by selling plates of chicken and didn't even have shorts to match our game jerseys.

But that didn't matter. I wanted to do everything I could to help the Port City Spokesmen reach their maximum potential. And that meant winning a national championship.

Though we had come into the tournament with some momentum, we were decided underdogs, and we relished that status. Unfortunately, the double-elimination tournament didn't start that well for us. Our first opponent, the Canadian National Team, blew us out of the gym as one of their players knocked down about 12 3-pointers. We were embarrassed and mad and started blaming each other. In sports, that's a surefire way to keep losing.

So, we stopped pointing fingers and instead formulated a game plan that would help us capitalize on our strengths. We had to regroup quickly because we had to play again first thing in the morning to fight to stay alive. And it wasn't going to get any easier—we would face teams that were sponsored by organizations such as the Miami Heat, Dallas Mavericks, and Cleveland Cavaliers.

Regardless, we started battling and winning. To crawl out of the loser's bracket, we had to win two or three games per day. The grueling schedule left our bodies beaten down. We didn't have the energy for parties or late nights at the clubs. Our hands were shredded. What used to be blisters were torn apart, and tender new-born skin was exposed.

One thing that I never got used to in my time around wheelchair ball is the smell of burning flesh. Sometimes, you're flying down the court and you have to stop to avoid a charge, to juke around a defender, or to just avoid crashing into a wall. Those thumbs and fingers are all you have to avoid disaster. The taut rubber tires are unforgiving, and you can almost see smoke from the friction as they skid across your skin.

But we are athletes. We block out the pain during the game and deal with it later. To make it through the next game and the next, I used athletic tape to completely encapsulate both thumbs and my index fingers, which acted as my brakes and my throttle.

The only thing that kept me pushing that chair was the competitive fire inside to help these guys win a National Championship.

For two exhausting days, every game was a potential elimination game. Somehow, we fought off every challenge and reached the finals where we faced the extremely organized and skilled Fort Wayne Bandits. Fort Wayne hadn't endured the difficult path to the championship like we had. We had already played seven games in four days. That's what happens when you lose your first game. We had to play the semifinal immediately prior to the championship that morning and the Bandits had almost a 24-hour break.

But we vowed that we would make no excuses. None. When it's all said and done, you are a champion or a forgettable second.

Fort Wayne looked intimidating with sharp, matching uniforms. Their layup lines were flawless. And here are the Port City Spokesmen, with no matching shorts and less finesse than a pit bull in a hammock. Heck, half of our players were older than their coach. We might have looked like the Bad News Bears of wheelchair ball, but we were tough as nails. We did not make the fanciest passes or light it up from the 3-point line. But we would bust your rear end in the paint, and when the game was over, your bruised and weary body would remind you that you faced a tough opponent.

Both teams bumped and scrapped and challenged every turn of every wheel. You could say both teams were worthy of a championship that day, but that's not how tournaments work. We don't share.

During the championship game, we physically bullied the Bandits. Through pure grit and determination, we wore down our opponents. We would not be denied. As our lead grew and it became evident that the Spokesmen were going to win a national championship, I looked around at Barrett and Tim and my other teammates and I thought, "I'm so happy for these guys." My mission had been to help my teammates win a National Championship.

I was humbled to share the moment with my teammates who had inspired me all season. What they consider routine everyday life was inspirational to me.

The buzzer sounded, and we had done the impossible. Our unknown, ragamuffin bunch of country boys from coastal North Carolina had accomplished a daunting feat that no one thought was possible. The crowd exploded around us and my teammates converged in pure joy and excitement. Hugs, high-fives, and tears were everywhere. I rolled slowly from under the goal toward center court where the masses were bunched, and the moment froze. It almost was like I heard nothing. Everything looked a little blurry and everyone was moving slowly.

I went from calm to very emotional. I was overcome with the realization of how rare this accomplishment was and that I played a part in this once-in-a-lifetime moment. I came to realize that I didn't just want this moment for my teammates. I also wanted this moment for Chad. I wiped the tears away from my cheeks with my filthy battered hands, leaving black smears on my face. I was undeniably proud.

Chapter 11: Family Means Everything

On Bended Knee

I'm not sure if you have already forgotten the super romantic night when I got into PT school, but the gorgeous brunette that bought me a drink that night wouldn't leave me alone!

I hope she doesn't read this . . . *I'm kidding*!!!

I know I would have been a fool to let her get away. Through graduate school and the start of my career, she was always by my side encouraging me to pursue my dreams.

After begging me to marry her . . . *OK, let me stop*!

As we stood atop a cruise liner in the Caribbean Sea, I asked for her hand on bended knee. A little more romantic, right? She blessed me by becoming my wife. Now we are fortunate to be raising two outstanding young men, and my family is my entire world. Everything I do is for them.

Des has been a huge supporter of my life and ever-changing ventures. Some wives might have caved in to the stress of my frequently changing careers and the uncertainty of a steady monthly stream of income. But since we were in our early 20s, Des has always provided the encouragement I needed to pursue my dreams. I can't imagine going through this life with anyone else by my side.

My sister, Elise, is also a huge part of my family's life. It's probably not common for adult siblings to be involved in each other's lives daily, but I'm glad that we are. We live in the same neighborhood and we get together almost every day. It's been amazing. My hectic schedule can be challenging for Des and me, so it's a great relief to know that Elise is there to help us. We are truly blessed.

Des and I have done everything we know how to do in order to be good parents. I have failed more times than I would like to admit to in being both a husband and parent, but my heart and intentions have always been true. Unfortunately, I haven't always followed my heart. We are all imperfect and that will always be a truth that most would care not to admit, but I believe that if we learn and grow from our mistakes than we are ahead of the pack. I am so thankful to have Des as a part of my life.

Our boys keep us on our toes, and I could not be prouder of anything in the world than being their dad. Like all families, we battle challenges but love always outweighs everything. I like to think that I am helping them to grow up to be great adults and not just good kids. Their personalities are so different, but so perfect for who they are becoming. I'm not going to brag all day on how incredible my kids are, but I tell them every single day how much they are loved.

I urge you to make sure you express unconditional love to your children no matter how tough the day has been, or how much they may have disappointed you, or how terrible their decision making has been. These are precisely the moments when they need to hear you express love the most. Sure, you have to correct and discipline them, but if they have no doubts that you love them more than anything in the world, they are more likely to abide by your wishes and learn from their mistakes.

Regardless of what happens, do not hold grudges toward your kids. Don't be tempted to shut off communication with them because of a disagreement or screw-up. Every situation is surmountable. Every disappointing moment can be redeemed. This also goes for how couples should express their love. Your spouse loves to hear that they are loved, and it's not always easy to say it and show it, but you must! Although it's "known" how much you love them, strive to express it in words and actions.

I know how incredibly blessed I was growing up to have two great examples of what parents should be. I do not take that for granted. I strive every day to be better and better. The challenges of parenting are endless, yet the rewards are irreplaceable. I will consider myself an extremely successful father if I am half the dad my father is.

I want to make sure that I give my kids everything they need, not necessarily everything they want. There is a huge discrepancy between the two. I want those boys to have a childhood like mine—reckless, open, confident, engaged. I want them to skin their knees and catch lizards and fall out of canoes. I want them to have great friends that will be part of the memories they cherish for the rest of their lives.

I want them to respect people, particularly those who are different than them. I want them to appreciate the differences between us.

I want them to love people no matter the differences that appear on the surface. I pray they crave giving back to those who are less fortunate and that they appreciate their gifts and blessings at all times. Living by example is terrifying at times. It's hard not to swear, or argue, or drink alcohol in excess when you just feel like letting loose. Sometimes, I have to remind myself to be the adult that I would be proud to see my kids become. I want them to see Desiree and me living as examples of good people and wanting to grow up to be like us, just as I wanted to emulate my parents.

I am not perfect and never will be but the urge to be closer to it is something I never lose. That's all we can truly ask of ourselves as children of God.

A Mother's Influence

I strive to be a father like my dad was to me. But I will never underestimate the influence my mom had on my development into a caring, understanding adult. Let me say this up front. My mother is the most selfless woman I know. She has a giver's heart.

My mom exemplified that throughout her professional career. For more than 25 years, Pam Porter taught children with special needs. You just don't wake up one day and think to yourself that special education seems like a pretty cool career. You have to have something special deep down in your core to excel in a field that tests your patience and presents enormous challenges on a daily basis.

Her classroom was unlike any other at Carroll Middle School. Her students ranged in age from 6 to sometimes 21 years of age. They had varying degrees of learning and physical disabilities—some would never be able to read a complete sentence; others couldn't form the words to ask a simple question.

She had some of the lowest abled kids that were allowed into the regular public-school system. Her job was to teach her students as much as they could possibly retain in order to prepare them for life. For some that would mean reading and simple math. But for most, their days would be filled with life skills such as cooking, cleaning, laundry, bathing, tying their shoes, verbalizing their thoughts, and working with simple tools. My mom helped them acquire many other skills, and no day was ever the same.

She taught many of the same kids for many years in a row, allowing her to form bonds with them far beyond the routine teacher-student relationship. Still to this day, she may bump into a former student at the grocery store or make house calls to see how they are doing. None of them ever forget Mrs. Porter. Her devotion to their well-being made a lasting impact on their lives, their family's lives, and on mine as well.

When the bell rang at the end of my day in middle school, I'd head to my mom's classroom, where I'd wait for a ride home. While I waited, I got to hang out with her students. Sometimes, I'd walk them to their destination, help them gather their things or push a wheelchair. But mostly, I'd talk to them and get to know them.

At that early age, I learned that it takes special teachers to work with special students. I also learned that most people of different abilities don't want to be treated differently. They want to be included, not singled out. They want to be spoken to just as you would speak to everyone else. I teased them the same way I'd tease my friends, and I'd crack jokes with them when they would do or say something silly. When I passed them in the hallway of the school, I always received a big smile and, often, a high-five. Because I was friendly to my mom's students, my friends became more comfortable interacting with them. I never saw this as anything special; it was just how human beings treat each other. For me, it wasn't a lesson I learned. Instead, my mom set the standard for how to treat people who look or act differently, and that behavior was ingrained in me at a young age.

The "R" word was absolutely forbidden at my mom's house long before the slogans ("Spread the word to end the word") came out and the movements began to remove the word from our vocabularies. Cursing wasn't allowed in my house ever but saying that other word around my mother was worse than slapping her in the face. Little did I realize that my mom's passion for these kids and adults would become a huge part of my adult life.

My soft spot for the special needs population showed up again during my classes at UNCW. I took an undergraduate class, Movement Considerations for Special Populations, with my favorite professor, Sue Combs. We learned to provide physical fitness activities and classes for those who needed extra assistance. In our "labs," we interacted and worked with some awesome kids. The experience was awkward and intimidating to most of my classmates, at least in the beginning, but I was completely comfortable, and I looked forward to every class.

Time passed, and careers began and changed. Through it all, I always felt compelled to help people who were less fortunate. I helped some inner-city youth through a Scouting program where we would entice the boys to show up on Saturdays to play basketball and we'd sneak in those core scouting principles along the way. Meeting and helping shape those kids was a rewarding experience, but I wanted more—something to lock my claws into and make a difference in my community.

The call came from a former professor from UNCW who wanted to introduce to me the concept of the Miracle League. I jumped in my truck and headed out to the outskirts of Wilmington to this empty field adjacent to a few softball fields. Dan Johnson shared his vision of a sports complex and baseball field that would be open and safe for people of all abilities to play together. I was excited to help build the foundation of this great facility and the programs that would call it home.

This baseball field would allow kids and adults with physical and mental disabilities to participate in baseball and softball games on a regulation field with their parents and friends cheering from the bleachers. The field—the turf, the base paths, the bases—are completely wheelchair-friendly, creating a zero-obstacle surface from the parking lot to the outfield fences.

The athletes who use the field range in ages from three to nearly 80. In the Miracle League, they are intermingled on ten teams. We have two competitive teams that are formed with our athletes who don't require our volunteer buddies to help them. We also have a "littles" game for our youngest players to play in, and it's the most adorable thing you have ever seen in your life!

The smiles. The hugs. The freedom. The pure joy. The excitement in the faces of both athlete and family member. The pride of accomplishment. Interacting in a real sport on a real team. None of this would have happened without the Miracle League.

As I stand in that rubber pitching circle, tossing ball after ball and trying to hit those bats, I think back to those lessons I learned from my mom.

Seeing these kids (and their devoted parents) work so hard to accomplish the simplest tasks is that occasional reminder we all need to not take things for granted. Even after my life-changing accident and even after playing basketball with the Port City Spokesmen, I sometimes forget to be thankful for all the things I can do—I can open my car door and drive across town, I can wrap my arms around my wife and kids, I can climb the stairs to my office, I can see all the colors of a sunrise over the Intracoastal Waterway.

It seems unfair at times that everyone can't do the same.

I can't give anyone new legs or new eyes. I can't go back in time and change the condition or event that caused them to never be able to walk.

All I can do is make the experience as normal as possible for the athletes. Isn't that what we all want in life, to feel included? So that's my volunteer job—to treat these Miracle League players like everybody else. That includes hugs, encouragement and pats on the back. But it also includes some good-natured teasing.

One day, one of my players was using her walker to get from third base to home plate.

"Come on, Bonnie!" I shouted. "You'd better move it or I'm gonna go get the ball and throw it at your rear-end!"

A visitor might have been appalled to witness an adult supporter telling someone using a walker to move their bottom. But the truth is that Bonnie had gone much faster before. She wasn't trying that hard, and as a friend and fan, I'm expected to encourage her to do her best.

I said it in a teasing voice, and sure enough, her smile broadened, and she picked up her pace for those final 25 feet.

It's the kind of normalcy these kids crave. They love the cheers and the hugs when they score a run. But they also love being challenged to do their best. These kids and adults put forth extraordinary effort every day just to adapt to the lives that we take for granted. So, we naturally try to make things as easy as possible for them. But sometimes, when we say, "You can do more. You can do better," it demonstrates that we know what they are capable of.

The Miracle League has changed lives of volunteers and athletes. For example, Mason, an amazing young man who has Down's Syndrome, had been attending his brothers' baseball games year after year without ever having an opportunity to play on his own team. Now his brothers attend his games and bring their teammates to come root for Mason. He lights up as the bat is placed in his hands, he swings with all his heart and takes off around the bases with his brothers running behind him, cheering him the whole way. Mason, you see, doesn't like to stop at first base; he goes all the way around the diamond every time he hits.

Just as my mom influenced me to accept all people just as they are, I feel like my sons have learned to reach out to those who are different. They join me in volunteering at Miracle League games, but they also make connections on their own.

My son Tatum's best buddy from school is the coolest dude around. Sincere was born visually impaired and can barely make out any objects. That doesn't stop him from being the funniest, wildest, worst dancing, 10-year-old I know! The dancing is a running joke with me and his momma. She says he dances more like my people, which I argue because some of us white people DO have rhythm.

I asked his mom one day if she thought he would be interested in coming out to the field one Saturday and trying out our league. Understandably, she was hesitant. She wanted him to play baseball with his classmates, so it was tough for her to accept that playing in the standard recreation leagues would grow more difficult as the kids got older and the games got more competitive. Sincere goes wide open on the playground with my son holding his hand and guiding him around safely, most of the time. But fast contact sports were a safety issue due to Sincere's limited eyesight. After a few invitations, she finally agreed to bring him out for a game. The rest is history, and the Miracle Field has become his happy place. Mom is so thrilled that she gets to watch from the bleachers as my son or another buddy helps guide Sincere around the field during the game. The big highlight is when he gets to crush the special Beeper Ball that I get to pitch to him.

The Beeper Ball makes special sounds, so our visually impaired players hear the ball as it gets closer. As Sincere tracked the sound of the ball, he learned to time his swing. He then found his way to the bases by way of beeper bases as well. It's a beautiful feeling to experience when you witness someone independently succeed at something they once thought unattainable.

The Miracle Field creates independence, instills pride and encourages accomplishment. It truly is a special place that is really like no other I have experienced. Take some time to find one near you. One afternoon could change your life.

Soldiers and Sequins

The Miracle League of Wilmington falls under the incredible umbrella of ACCESS of Wilmington. I could not be prouder and more humbled to sit as the Board Chair because there is no more perfect match for me. We provide the opportunities for fitness, recreation, athletics, team sports, and wellness for anyone who has limitations or boundaries keeping them from participating otherwise. This includes opportunities for people with any form of disability. We are a one-stop shop for adaptive activity.

Our SOAR Program provides opportunities for our veterans, and it's wonderful to be able to help them return to a more normal life post-injury and disability. I always assumed there were dozens of programs that helped our disabled vets get back to an active life, but I was mistaken. Sadly mistaken. Often, they are almost forgotten once they are no longer an active part of the military world. Many vets who have been through our program describe feeling abandoned once they are medically stable to live on their own or with their families. Living isn't enough. Surviving and getting by is not enough. They deserve the same opportunities as you and me. These men and women risked life and limb for the safety and security of our country.

Sometimes, when people see my prostheses, they mistakenly assume that I'm a soldier who was injured in an act of war. I correct them immediately, because I know the sacrifices our wounded veterans have made. The bravery and honor they exhibit is unparalleled. A few times, I have been out to eat with my family, and my dinner has been paid for by a generous, anonymous stranger, who left a "Thank you for your service" message with the waitstaff. If the stranger is out the door, all I can do is accept the meal on behalf of my family. And then, the next time I see a veteran at a booth across a restaurant, I forward the good deed to that family.

At SOAR, we are proud to reach out to veterans and offer them the help they deserve.

And we also cater to those who like to play dress up.

One of my favorite events ever, the I Am Beautiful Fashion Show, began as a hopeful concept and brainchild of a wonderful young lady named Angela. I was excited to be asked to be a part of the very first show. The concept is brilliantly simple. Put on a live fashion show, feature the most beautiful models we can find to wow our audience, and raise money for some deserving nonprofits, including ACCESS.

Fashion shows to raise money for nonprofits isn't an original concept. Lots of people like to get glammed up and watch the models sashay down the runway. If you know me, though, you know these types of *frou-frou* events aren't really my thing. I would choose Carhartt over Versace any day, but still, I love to get dressed up in my tuxedo for this one fashion show.

Yes, this fashion show includes the typical adornments. The stunning dresses and slick menswear, the flashes of the cameras everywhere you turn, all of the diva experiences of professional hair and makeup, the bass pumping from the DJ booth, and the spotlights accenting the runway that's surrounded on three sides with the most excited and boisterous crowd you've ever seen.

The difference is . . . our beautiful models will probably never grace the cover of *Cosmopolitan* magazine. Every one of our models lives with some form of a disability. However, for one night, they have the opportunity to show everyone how beautiful they truly are.

In a few short years, we put on six fashion shows. What started as a fledgling project with 12 models has grown into a standing room only event with nearly 60 models. The atmosphere is electric and filled with the purest smiles. In the hours before the big night, I get to watch these special people take a trial spin down the runway. Some are shy or nervous; others embrace the attention. Before the show, I get to sit with them, relaxing them and instilling confidence.

Just as I am about to announce their names and signal them to start their trip down the runway, I get to look into their eyes and see the excitement bubbling up inside of them. When they emerge from behind the curtain, the crowd cheers and screams and takes photos, and you can see that our models are realizing a dream of feeling like the most beautiful person in the world. When you think of the difficulties they might have faced or the names they might have been called, it's an absolute blessing to be able to help them feel this great. The audience recognizes it, too, as evidenced by the watery eyes around the room. And me? I can almost feel the arm hairs poking through my tuxedo from the chills I feel.

Sometimes, I wish I could capture those warm, fuzzy feelings every day. Some days, I need a break from travel agents and politicians and the everyday adult life that can spoil a good mood.

So, I escape to Bitty & Beau's coffee shop. You see, some of our Miracle League athletes and I Am Beautiful models work at the coffee shop. A staff of 40 workers with developmental and intellectual disabilities greet guests, serve coffee and provide spontaneous entertainment at the drop of a dance beat. These are my people, the ones who inspire me to be a better person.

Not surprisingly, a good portion of this book was written at Bitty & Beau's, which gained national attention through appearances on the *Rachael Ray Show* and when founder and mother of Bitty and Beau, Amy Wright, was awarded CNN's 2017 Hero of the Year Award. Amy became a pioneer when she opened a coffee shop that employs a staff with developmental and intellectual disabilities almost exclusively.

Bitty & Beau's has since expanded to Charleston, S.C., and Savannah, Ga., and Amy intends to share this joyous concept with other cities. If you ever visit one of these iconic southern cities, please stop by. I guarantee you'll be greeted with a smile, and you'll take one home with you.

When I see the sponsorships on the walls at the Miracle Field and at Bitty & Beau's, I am reminded how awesome my community is. Your community can do this, too. Those children and adults with disabilities deserve to feel special.

And if you don't believe me, just ask my mom.

Chapter 12:
Telling My Story

Stage of Innocence

As most of you are aware by now, I spend my career traveling the globe speaking and striving to inspire others. I am so blessed to have the absolute best job in the world. What you might not know is that it took months, years, even decades for me to achieve this perfect scenario. From my first lucid moments in the hospital following the accident, I have never shied away from telling someone what happened to me and describing it in as much detail as they wanted.

Initially, I just shared my story with friends, mostly because they were the ones who asked. The first few years after the accident, I was still writing my story every day as I overcame a new hurdle or learned a new insight about living as an amputee. I was in no position to tell my story as I was still learning what good could be generated from such a tragic situation.

I had always been a cut-up and a "ham," as we say in the south. I was dangerously obsessed with entertaining and making people laugh. Before I was even 2 years old, my people-pleasing antics led me straight to the hospital and under the knife! Yes, I ended up in major surgery just from trying to entertain. As a toddler, I was just beginning to move quickly. So, I used to run through the living room—or wherever I could find an audience— and leap into the air with my feet and legs straight out and land on my bottom. *I never said I was blessed with common sense.* Yes, I would simply run and jump and land right on my butt. My sicko parents and their friends found it hilarious, and laughter fueled me.

I suppose you could say I was performing physical comedy way before Chris Farley destroyed *Saturday Night Live* sets as the motivational speaker who lives in a van down by the river. I would continue to do it as long as the adults would pay attention to me. Come to find out, all those crash landings proved to be bad for the internal organs. Before I was out of diapers, I had to have emergency hernia surgery.

Shyness was never much of an issue for me. I was a borderline showoff. No, I can't sit here and lie to you nice people . . . *I was a total showoff!* And my preschool hernia surgery was just the first of many trips to the emergency room. At about eight years old, I was showing off as a real-life Superman jumping from table to table in the church fellowship hall. After several successful leaps, I misjudged the distance between the last two tables, and unfortunately, my chin caught the corner of the table. Emergency room. Stitches.

Another time I was thrilling the neighborhood crew, at about age 10, flying down the hill on my bike, turning the handle bars side to side, just to show them how super cool I was. But then I turned the tire just a little too far, abruptly stopping the bike and sending me flying over the handles. With my hands still gripped tightly to the bike, my helmetless head cushioned my landing as I ended up in a scorpion pose on the asphalt. Every mom within earshot of my scream ran out of their homes, elbowing each other for a chance to pour peroxide, alcohol, and Mercurochrome all over my gaping head wound. Emergency room. Stitches.

I loved to entertain others, and sometimes the story did not end in the emergency room. My outgoing personality compelled me to audition for lead roles in church and school plays, and I often landed them. So, speaking and being on stage was extremely comfortable for me. But that wasn't really Chad on stage. That was a comedian, a character. I had never been as vulnerable and personal as I would have to be when I was asked to tell my story publicly for the first time.

A Glimpse of the Future

That opportunity arose my senior year in high school. Our energetic, motivated youth group was a blessing in many ways to me as a kid growing up. Being in a positive environment around generally good kids helped to keep me grounded and headed in a positive direction. As a yearly tradition, the youth of the church led all aspects of one Sunday service each spring. We taught Sunday School, greeted parishioners, took up the offering, and led the hymns. This was a big deal for the youth and also for the congregation, who appreciated a change of pace.

I always was excited for Youth Sunday. As we grew into teenagers, we were given increasingly more responsibility. I had progressed through the years from just being part of the choir to lighting the candles. During my junior year, I read some scripture during the service and taught the "little old ladies" Sunday school class. That wasn't the official name, but I loved teaching that class because they LOVED me. I am smart enough to realize that they didn't love me for my ability to convey the teachings of the Bible in a way they had never experienced, but rather because I was a cute boy who reminded them of their grandsons. It didn't matter for one second what came out of my mouth. They probably didn't hear a word I said . . . literally.

As much as I loved the "little old ladies," the real highlight for me was the opportunity to be co-preacher for that day's service. Yes, the pinnacle of Youth Sunday. I spent weeks preparing my speech, so that I could attain the same level of competence as my longtime buddy Dayton Wilson. Dayton always had a gift for public speaking and a conviction for the Word, so it's not surprising that he has earned a Master of Divinity and is now a Presbyterian pastor!

I knew immediately upon being selected to speak that I wanted to include my story that morning. I had discovered a few scriptures to sprinkle into my story because that's what preachers do, right? I'm not sure how well I incorporated them that day, but for the first time I told my story in public. Many people in the congregation knew bits and pieces about the accident, the horror that followed, and my subsequent recovery. But only my mom and dad knew the whole story.

I was a little nervous at the start, and I had a long series of notes to read from, but once I got going, the notes became irrelevant. The story gained passion the less I looked down and the more I could make eye contact with the audience who seemed to be clinging to every word. I wasn't a great speaker, but their interest had less to do with my delivery that day and more with the experience of sharing something impactful. I figured out that some people needed to hear that message, but I had no clue how many it would be.

I never saw what I went through as anything amazing. Sure, I had difficult times, but I was so focused on getting my life back that I was almost oblivious to my own challenges and accomplishments. An observer could be awestruck at my attitude, my dedication and my perseverance. But to me, every roadblock was just one more challenge I had to overcome. That's why I never thought playing basketball would be regarded as such an inspirational achievement. But to those who watched me accomplish what few others in the world had ever done, the experience was special. The same thing rang true for this specific Sunday. I was just trying to make it through my twenty minutes without forgetting my lines or using bad grammar. Preaching on Youth Sunday was sort of a high school bucket list item for me. But it became much more.

I cannot tell you how it felt to be in the pews that day, but the responses I received were overwhelming. On a normal Sunday, the congregation would virtually sprint to their cars at high noon to beat the Baptists and Methodists to Western Sizzlin or one of the other restaurants we had in our small town. But the crowd hung around that day to chat with both me and Dayton along with the rest of the youth and our families. It was a different kind of day. The parishioners stopped to tell me how impactful the message was and how they needed to hear it. But then they did something I was totally unprepared for. They started telling me their own stories of struggle and faith and the challenges they were facing.

I was stunned. I was just a high school kid telling my story. Yet, these adults, a generation or two older than me, told me how my sharing inspired them to work on their problems or helped them move on from an issue that was holding them down. I really felt like I was helping people. Maybe, I thought, something special had just happened.

One day later, the *Robesonian*, our local newspaper, received an audio recording from the service and took the liberty to transcribe it into their paper. Word for word, my speech was there in black and white for all to see. My heart. My soul. My vulnerable story. Readers overwhelmed me with requests to tell my story in front of their churches and youth groups. Each time I spoke, I was greeted by more stories and more hugs and more mascara smeared on my oxford cloth shirts. I loved every second of it.

The experience took me back to the worst day of my life; the day I lost all hope. That day I wanted to end my life. I asked "why" a thousand times and heard the voice that forever changed the course of Chad Porter's life.

"Don't worry, you'll find out."

"Don't worry, you'll find out."

Yes, those words helped stop the flooding of tears and the screams of heartache. They helped me regain a fragment of hope. They helped me focus on what I needed to accomplish, and supplied the drive and willpower it would take. Those words changed my life. They were so vague. Less than what I wanted, but just what I needed.

I had no clue what was meant by those words, but I was determined to find out.

I knew on that faith-filled Youth Sunday that I had my WHY.

Finding My Why

I am extremely fortunate to understand my why. At least the why in my life that pertains to my accident. There are many more occasions where I haven't found the why. We all ask why, and many times, our answers are never understood. I wish I could answer your questions of why things happen in your life. I wish I could ease your pain and relieve your hurt with some philosophical answer.

But I don't have that answer. I can only explain my journey of how I found my why. It may sound simple, because it was revealed to me the day I spoke in church and touched so many lives, but it took many years past that point to really grasp how I feel life works and how it corresponds to God's promises. I'm not saying I have it all figured out either. I question things all the time. I struggle to understand, and yet my faith always eases my anxiety.

We have to go back to that Thursday night just three and a half weeks post-accident. I was in the hospital room, alone, having just watched the "inspiring" video. You remember. *Why?! Why me?!* Growing up in the church, I was always told that God has huge plans for you. You only need to trust Him and seek your purpose through Him.

As a teenager, I wasn't walking the hallways of the school or busting my rear on the courts and fields consciously seeking out God's plan for myself. I was enjoying life and thought that once I was older, then I could take this stuff more seriously. I was sure God would just clearly pave the way for me and there would be no doubt what His plan was.

Then came the accident, and that revelatory night in the hospital. I was so mad at God that night. I had given my life to Him. I did what

He asked of me. Why did He do this to me? You've asked that, I know. Was this His grand plan? Did He make that boat run over me to kick-start His plan for my life? Did He put me and my family and friends through months and years of pain and suffering for His own purposes? Some of these questions surfaced that night. Some over the years to come. But they were always in the back of my mind.

Yes, things worked out well for me. Yes, I am able to help people on a daily basis and it's a true blessing. But that still left me with questions. I knew that I had become a better person and my life had been shaped to serve and help people, but was this all a plan? Quite cryptic for the Maker of the Heavens and the Earth. Wouldn't it have been easier if He would have just somehow spoken to me as I was in church one day or had His face appear on my morning toast?

Fast forward to almost twenty-two years later. I decided to take my Emmaus Walk. If you aren't familiar with this, I will give you the abbreviated version.

The walk to Emmaus is an experience of Christian spiritual renewal and formation that begins with a three-day short course in Christianity. It is an opportunity to meet Jesus Christ in a new way as God's grace and love is revealed to you through other believers. It can be a very powerful weekend. You certainly leave feeling loved.

Amongst all the love and support and highs of the weekend, an unexpected realization came to light for me.

Understand that I am and have been for all these years 100% comfortable and happy with my life and the course that it has taken.

We had the opportunity to write down a question that the pastor and spiritual leaders would answer or at least try to answer in front of the group. I sat for a moment, trying to think of something I wanted answered. Ummm . . . Ummmm . . . Wait, I have a question! I started writing and kept writing and I had to flip the small piece of paper over to finish my thought. It was like someone was dictating to me or moving my hand for me.

The leader of the group was reading the questions and had quick theological answers for all of them. Then he got to mine . . .

I've heard all my life that God has a plan for our lives and that he's had this plan for us since before birth. If He has our entire life planned, then obviously my getting run over by a boat was in His plan. Was getting devastated by a propeller all part of God's grand plan for my life?

Emmaus walks involve several pastors who serve as spiritual council for moments just like these. I was convinced for the past twenty-two years that this WAS in God's plan for me and I was completely at peace with that fact. I had the opportunity to speak with each of the pastors that day and I have asked others since and nearly all of them gave me the same answer.

God doesn't make bad things happen to you!

Life just happens sometimes, and not everything has an explanation. But one thing is certain: To those who believe in Him, God can make some amazing things happen out of the worst circumstances.

It makes sense. God doesn't force us to live a certain way and make the decisions that He would. He allows us all free will. We have the freedom to do whatever we please, the good, the bad, and everything in-between. Free will allows us to choose our own pathways. I have often wished that I did not have the responsibility to choose my own way because I have screwed it up so many times. I bet you have as well. Because He gives us free will, it doesn't mean He approves our decisions. We are entrusted to make our own choices, so we bear the responsibility to make the right ones.

Bad things will happen, and many won't make sense, but we must have faith that His promises to us are real. He sent His Son to earth to touch the world and be a living, breathing form of God. He never promised that following Him would be easy or cause your trials to fade away, but He promised to be with you, and without that relationship, what do you have?

I'm always perplexed by those who don't believe in God. Where do they draw their strength, faith, and hope from? What gives them purpose to keep fighting? My self-inflicted mistakes combined with those I don't have control over are hard to cope with even though I know I am unconditionally loved and forgiven. God promises that He will help us through life, and at the end of our journey, we will get to spend eternity in the most wonderful place imaginable. Without Him, navigating this life is extremely tough.

True Calling

I have always been driven by a desire to help others. I have tried to find jobs where I could serve others and still support my family. The careers I chose seem diverse, but they all had a common thread—I was helping others.

Pursuing physical therapy was a no-brainer. I could help others overcome their physical and emotional challenges, just like so many amazing people had done for me after my accident.

Being a physical therapist was a rewarding career, but I had an insatiable entrepreneurial spirit and my desire to work for myself dominated my thoughts. I wanted to have my own practice. Unfortunately, seventy-five percent of PT (physical therapy) patients come from orthopedic medicine practices, and already have therapists in place. Most of the other larger groups were building one-stop-shops that included in-house physical therapy. The financial risk of starting a practice from scratch was more than I was ready to take.

After I had worked at the rehab hospital for a little over four years, I decided to start a new chapter in my life.

I left PT and delved into real estate, and welcomed the opportunity to learn about sales. I had always felt that I could sell anything, but I had never been tested. I learned very quickly that it takes a lot of work to be successful, and far more attributes than just a purty face.

What I loved about my time selling raw land homesites was the understanding that a sale done correctly has nothing to do with selling anything. Successful sales people solve problems and fulfill needs. The art of asking questions and listening to clients' desires always leads you to the tools necessary to get them what they want or need.

One key to my growth in real estate sales came from being introduced to a man who would make a large impact on my career and my life. Almost every sales meeting included at least one slide with words of wisdom from this guru. As I read and listened to his material, I learned why he was extremely influential.

Mr. Zig Ziglar. This guy was awesome. I loved his way of motivating and teaching with storytelling and brilliant anecdotes. At the time, I had no idea that his influence on my life would carry far beyond my days in real estate.

After a few years in real estate, I felt driven again to seek out a different way to serve people and still make enough money to take care of my family. I was inspired by my Uncle Joe. Not long after Desiree and I were married, my Uncle Joe met with us to help us get our "affairs in order." I figured I already had things in order. At the time, I was a physical therapist working at a hospital with good benefits and a retirement plan. I had no clue what it meant to really take care of my situation as an adult and as a husband and father.

Joe had worked in financial services for over forty years, and he showed us how to make sure our family was protected should something ever happen to me or Des. I felt a sense of relief after meeting with Uncle Joe. So, as I was leaving real estate, I loved the idea of helping people the way my uncle had helped my family.

A year later and after many, many hours at the local library studying incessantly and taking numerous exams, I earned my license to help families with their financial and insurance needs. I expected the new gig to be a breeze since I was using the amazing system that my uncle had perfected, in addition to my finely-honed sales skills. Ummmm . . . . *Not so much.*

Starting Porter Financial was harder than I ever imagined. Serving the clients' needs wasn't that difficult, but pulling in new clients was a real challenge. There is no down time for an independent salesman. If you expect to succeed, you are always prospecting to keep the pipeline full. Don't get me wrong. I did fine financially, and I was grateful to be able to help many families, but financial planning was as challenging as it was rewarding.

While I was growing Porter Financial, I received a nudge from a friend. My older son Tatum was in elementary school, and the friend suggested I visit Tatum's class during October, which is Disability Awareness Month. He said I should show my leg to the kids and tell them my story. I thought it was a great idea, although I knew I'd have to tone down the graphic imagery for the squeamish. My trip to Tatum's class was more of a show and tell. I let them touch the prosthetic leg and ask questions.

What a great day it was! The engagement and inquisitiveness of Tatum's classmates created another one of those moments when my "why" was reconfirmed. Later that day, I posted a picture with the kids on social media, and a flood of messages ensued.

The consensus was: "Please come to our school and talk to our kids; they need to hear a positive message and be encouraged." The requests covered all levels of students from elementary school to college. Of course, I can't say "no" to the kids. So, I dusted off my vocal cords and started developing the presentations again.

What an amazing feeling it was to be sharing my story again and providing a little nugget of hope and faith that so many kids needed. Before long, I was standing in front of an auditorium full of 700 middle school children, helping them to believe that no matter what they are going through, there is always a way through it. These are kids who insist they are okay, and that they don't need help. But their eyes tell a different story. Sometimes, I would see the toughest-looking kids in the room fight back a tear. And if I was fortunate, I'd get a chance to talk to them one-to-one. My only goal was to help them to not give up and inspire them to seek help from those who support and love them.

Those impactful moments rekindled my desire to share my story. When you connect with a wounded soul, you feel buoyed by invincible hope. In that moment, you want to devote your entire life to making connections and helping others.

I felt drawn once again to my calling. But this calling had to be balanced very carefully with my obligation as a husband and a father to support my family. I wanted to speak every day and travel to distant places and share my story with people who had never heard of Chad Porter.

But I had to stay grounded. I had three mouths to feed and lights to keep on.

Over the next year, more and more opportunities arose to speak for groups, including corporations and adult church groups. I built my own website to see if I could reach other groups who could benefit from hearing an inspirational message. As I fielded more and more requests to speak, I researched professional speaking.

I was convinced that professional speaking would be the most rewarding career choice I could ever imagine. But I still had to support my family through Porter Financial, and I wasn't confident enough to sacrifice my practice for this "dream." At least, not yet!

I started marketing myself on websites that hosted speakers and helped match you with prospective audiences. Every time I spoke to a group . . . an elementary school, a military group, or a group of employees, I would get one or two referrals. And that meant hundreds more would hear my message of perseverance and faith.

I continued to balance my days between marketing my speaking business with taking care of my financial clients, but my fire had been re-ignited for speaking. I realized very quickly that pursuing my passion wasn't just a dream. You don't have to be a former CEO of some huge company to make a living speaking.

In my first year of speaking, I gave it about fifty percent of my weekly effort, and I spoke to thirty-five groups. They didn't all pay a professional fee, and I sometimes paid more for food, travel and lodging than I received in compensation. But that was okay. I was sharing a message, touching people's lives, honing my delivery, and building a reputation. Since that first year, I have averaged 50-60 events per year.

God is good.

Chapter 13:
Always a Reason to Live

Unexplained Tears

For many years, I have had the chance to speak to youth all over the country. I have had the privilege of hearing countless stories from kids—some that are so inspiring and some that will break your heart.

A few years ago, I was speaking at a middle school and after my hour in front of about 600 students, one young lady was pulled over to me by a couple of friends. Clutching the hands of her friends, she was visibly emotional and never broke eye contact as she approached me. Her friends had no idea why she had tears running down her cheeks; they just knew that she needed to talk to someone. The gym emptied as students began to make their way back to their classrooms. The beautiful young girl's friends left her standing in front of me. I looked at her and said, "Would you like to sit down and talk?" She just nodded her head affirmatively.

One of the coaches allowed me to use an office so we could quietly chat. I had no clue what was about to come out of her mouth. She began to tell me how sad she was and how she didn't think she was going to make it.

Let me paint the picture. She was a tall, super cute, athletic-looking seventh-grade girl with no reason whatsoever to feel self-conscious. Underneath it all, though, she was hurting very deeply. "Sometimes I feel like I don't want to live anymore," she said. She told me she had been bullied for a couple years and had been shunned by girls that used to be her best friends. The pain overtook the joy in her life, and she couldn't see a reason to endure all the pain anymore. She couldn't see all the positives that were part of her life. A stranger like me could see all the positive attributes the young lady possessed, yet they felt nonexistent to her.

I sat with her and listened attentively. I tried not to say anything, just so she could get all these feelings off her chest.

After she had expressed her sadness and pain, I finally spoke. "Who knows how you feel?"

"No one," she said.

"Have you told your parents how you feel?"

"No way. I don't want to worry them." she said.

Let that sink in for a second. She didn't want to tell her parents about how badly she was suffering because she didn't want to worry them. She didn't want to upset them. Wow! I was speechless. But at the same time, I understood.

Your kids won't always come to you when they are in their worst pain and going through their biggest challenges. This a hard truth to swallow. It would devastate me to think that my boys wouldn't come to me if they needed me. One of my main goals as a parent is to have a deep relationship with my boys so that they will turn to me in times of need. I want them to feel like they can tell me anything. I believe there are ways of strengthening trust and helping my kids know they have someone they can come to in these moments.

Sometimes, teens and tweens feel like their problems are trivial and not worth bothering anyone about. Often, they are embarrassed to tell anyone for the risk of being judged or told they brought their troubles on themselves. More times than not, they don't think anyone, particularly an adult, will understand. Some convince themselves that they are alone, and no one can help them.

Some feel they can handle their problems on their own. *I can get through this. I am strong enough to handle my own emotions.*

Kids do not have the tools to navigate these tough situations on their own. So, what can we do as parents or friends of young people to make them comfortable enough to reach out to us? There's not one answer for every situation, but maybe you can start the conversation in your own home and build trust. Working together, you can hash out solutions before a small problem becomes insurmountable.

My advice to parents: Listen to your kids so intently that they will choose to talk to you about everyday happenings. Let them know they are the most important people in the world. I don't care how silly or immature it sounds. If it's worth them talking to you about, it's worth listening to with a caring ear. Start listening as soon as they form their first words and continue listening with your heart throughout their lives.

If they choose to tell you about something that is going on in their lives, or about something they may have done, right or wrong, you need to stop everything and listen. I know you are busy and have "more important" things to do, but I promise you that there is nothing more important than showing your kids that you care. Those conversations about SpongeBob will turn into girlfriend/boyfriend questions that will turn into wanting to know your opinion about sex and alcohol. If you have taken the time to be there to listen and be supportive about all the other things in your children's lives, when the tough times come around, they will be more apt to talk to you. If you dismissed the silly stuff, those conversations from the early years, they may not confide in you when they really need your support.

Permanent Decisions

March 24th, 2017 is a day I will never forget. Our church's youth director called, clearly distraught and incomprehensible. I could only decipher a few words: "Cody has taken his life." I wish I could explain what went through my mind, but I cannot put that feeling into words.

I have no clue what came out of my mouth. I was in disbelief. How? Why? What happened? This cannot be true!

Cody was a caring, 15-year-old boy in our youth group. When I first met him, he was a quiet, shy kid dressed in camouflage from head to toe. His father and stepmother would drive him nearly an hour one way just so he could hang out with the great kids in our youth group. As Cody became more comfortable with our group, he grew less reserved, and getting him to *stop* talking became the challenge! As I got to know Cody and his parents, I learned that he had his share of struggles in school. Cody was also a fighter, not in the sense of a physical brawler, but he had overcome his share of challenges as a young child.

His father and stepmother provided amazing direction and support. They gave love and support and did everything possible to create the best environment for the children. Cody's happy spot was at our church. He loved him some Jesus and never hid from it.

Here's the part that is so baffling. Cody had been doing really well. He had just gotten back from a spring youth retreat where he had a great time. Then, just a few days later he ended his life. It rocked everyone's world.

We look for explanations when things like this happen. We try to make sense of it. We try to justify his reasoning. Sometimes, though, there are no answers. We don't know what brought him to that moment, and we don't understand how God could let it happen. We each try to find something to cling to in order to move forward, but we are just grasping at thin air. Sometimes there is no answer.

Being the people pleaser that he was, I know Cody wouldn't want anyone sitting around crying for him. He did not leave a letter to explain why he felt he couldn't go on living. When the sheriff's deputies searched Cody's room, they found one letter of interest. The letter had no signature. No date. But the letter appeared to be a thank you letter to Cody from a young girl. What's so ironic about this letter is that she was thanking him for talking her out of killing herself. He had been a beacon of hope for this young girl and was able to listen and help her out of her situation. How amazing is that? Amazing, yet even more baffling. Why did Cody convince this young girl that her life was worth living, yet he didn't feel the same about his own?

I understand the level of despair a person can get to where they feel like life is no longer worth living. After my accident, I had feelings like that myself. It's always hard to understand why someone would choose this route in their lives, unless you have been there yourself. The void of all hope is debilitating. It can develop from years of unfortunate circumstances or come very quickly when you can't see past the nightmare that has become your life. I understand.

All the adults in Cody's life had our own questions and heartbroken feelings, but we needed to be strong for his family and our devastated youth.

What do you say to the parents? The only thing I could muster up was, "We are here for anything you may need. You are loved and have unlimited support." I had nothing else to offer.

We, the youth group leaders, were dealing with our own grief when we had to confront the question we couldn't answer: What do we say to our youth?

They look to us for answers. They expect us to be able to make them feel better and give them some clarity. The wrong phrase could glorify the situation, so I knew we needed to be very careful.

After the death of a loved one, we sympathize with their grief and point out any positives that come to mind. For those who've lost a chronically sick or elderly relative, I've often said, with conviction: "They are in a better place. At least they aren't hurting anymore."

But suicides are very different. We don't want our youth to think that suicide is a viable solution to their pain. I don't want them rationalizing that *Cody is in Heaven and he is pain-free.* Cody's friends were in pain, too. They wanted to extinguish their pain as well. They wanted to be in a better place. So, the conversation is precarious.

We wanted to ease our kids' minds that Cody was in heaven with God and he was okay. Many were worried that Cody choosing to take his own life was considered the ultimate sin and was unforgivable by God. Nothing in the Bible says that, however, and we wanted the kids to know that Cody knew God and had accepted him as his personal Savior many years prior.

A cloud hung over our church for days. We wiped tears, hugged shoulders and spoke in muted tones. Dark times and moments can overwhelm even the strongest among us, but Cody's parents never wavered in their faith. The grace that his family showed during this time strengthened everyone. I asked Cody's family if I could mention his story in the book. When they learned that I asked because I truly believe Cody's story might somehow save the life of another teen or help someone who is grieving a tragic loss, they readily agreed. It's a hard story to tell, but I pray it helps make a difference.

One of Cody's Sunday School teachers shared with me that Cody had begun to write a book. He privately shared it with her one Sunday. His collection of folded papers formed the shape of a book, and his words filled the pages. The book was his story. He wrote about the challenges he endured as a child and some of the things he had to overcome. Remember, this is a 15-year-old kid. His teacher asked why he was writing this book. He looked her straight in the eyes, and said seriously, "I want kids to read my story, so it can help someone who has gone through what I have."

How cool is this kid? He is missed and will not be forgotten. To help fulfill Cody's dream, I am going to try and reach those who may be on the verge of suicide. Just like he was. Just like that beautiful seventh-grade girl was.

And just like 15-year-old Chad Porter was.

We must first acknowledge that teen suicide exists, and that no demographic is immune. It affects every community, and it crosses the mind of more teens than you can imagine. I remember asking a group of about 200 high school kids, with their eyes closed and heads down, to raise their hands if they had ever considered taking their lives. About half of the room raised their hands. I was blown away. I knew that teen suicide was prevalent, but my eyes were opened to an epidemic. I studied suicide and learned that it is the second leading cause of death of kids between the ages of 12 and 18. Research indicates there are over 5,240 suicide attempts per year in the same age group. More teenagers die from suicide than from cancer, heart disease, AIDS, birth defects, stroke, pneumonia, influenza, and chronic lung disease, combined.

Suicide? Not My Kid

It will never happen to our kid because . . .

- Our kid is loved . . .
- Our kid goes to church . . .
- Our kid is a good athlete . . .
- Our kid is super talented . . .
- Our kid doesn't hang out with the wrong crowd . . .

Suicide rocks families every day that feel the exact same way, and they never see it coming. Sometimes, there are signs.

- Irritability
- Loss of interest in social activities
- Changes in appetite
- Unusual sleep patterns
- Loss of energy
- Excessive boredom
- Self-degrading comments
- Poor performance or frequent absences in school
- Comments about the world or someone being better off without them or believing that life is meaningless

If we recognize these signs, we can address depression, try to open the lines of communication and get these teens to express what's going on.

The catch is that almost all of these signs can also be normal reactions to being a teenager. The ambiguity complicates diagnosing teen depression and can be a reason why it goes unrecognized and untreated. Parents can also be ashamed to acknowledge that their teen is depressed. But having a child with some degree of depression isn't necessarily a reflection of your success as a parent. Don't think you have failed as a parent, and don't let your ego keep you from getting help for your child. If you think your teen might be depressed, ask for professional help or guidance.

A law enforcement officer recently told me that our community was lucky because we have had very low teen suicide numbers. He knows the statistics, so that's good.

A little later that night I thought about the suicides I had heard about over the last year or two. I'm sure the families, teachers and friends of the teens who did take their lives are not comforted by any statistics. Because ONE is too many. For one teen to feel so hopeless is a tragedy. The pain that child experienced and the loss and sadness that now consumes their family are very real despite what the statistics may say.

When Cody took his life, teen suicide hit closer to home than I had ever experienced. I have surrounded myself with youth in my life at church, in schools I speak to, and athletic teams that I spend time with. I do my best to reach as many kids as I can.

I know that God has a plan for every one of these young people. Their lives are full of promise and potential, and they might not know it.

So, I do my best to make sure that every kid I see takes home an important message. Sometimes, I grab them by the cheeks and look into their eyes and urge them to do one thing for me when times get tough . . . .

Don't make a permanent solution to a temporary problem.

There is no problem that you are dealing with that you cannot get through. Nothing. No matter how insurmountable your obstacle may seem, there is nothing that you can't overcome. I know it feels like the weight of the earth is on you and that you aren't strong enough to take another step. I know it feels like you have been treated unfairly and that no one understands what you are going through. It feels easier just to quit. It feels like no one will miss you. The pain is unbearable, and it feels like it will never get any better. All these feelings you have are understandable. I have experienced some of those same feelings.

I may not have experienced your situation and I will not tell you that I understand what you are going through. But I will tell you I know how bad it hurts to think about ending it. You are NOT alone. I promise you. You are never alone.

I hope after reading to this point that you know now that you don't have to take this journey alone. You have people who can help you. What scares me is that when you are in that state of depression that you lie to yourself and convince yourself differently. Your problems are NOT PERMANENT. They will pass. I can't be any more emphatic about that.

There might be more painful days ahead, but it all will pass. The choice is yours to fight or give up.

Taking your own life is permanent and robs you of everything. In the darkest of moments there will be a sunrise the next day. What seems so bad right now may turn out to be what catapults you into something amazing.

When I suffered a horrific injury and had my leg amputated, I felt like it was the end of my life as I knew it. For 15 years, my identity was Chad Porter, the athlete. I was working toward earning a college scholarship and possibly even a professional sports career. In 15 seconds, everything I had accomplished and hoped to accomplish in the future was taken from me. I would never have my life back again. I felt like I had no purpose, no value, and no reason to live.

It was real. Real pain. Real feelings. Real life at that moment in time. I couldn't see past the pain and darkness. I saw no future. I had no clue where my life would eventually lead.

Had it not been for God's promise to never leave my side, I would have given up. I'm so thankful for him telling me that night, "Don't worry, you'll find out."

You weren't created to be a failure. You weren't born to be unhappy. We are all purposefully made to do amazing things. Without exception.

You can decide how you will get there. Everyone has challenges. Some feel like they are much harder than others but just like no one knows everything you go through; you don't know theirs either. So, don't just assume no one else is going through similar things.

Don't think you can deal with this on your own. No one is equipped to deal with these things alone. Ask for help. It's nothing to be ashamed of. You are worthy of a full life. Don't let a bump in the road convince you otherwise.

Filtered Messages

The youth of this world have always needed help, support, and encouragement. From the Great Depression to the those growing up in the Hippie '60s, the children of every era have endured unique challenges.

Entire generations grew up so poor that they didn't know if there would be a meal on the table tomorrow or the next day. A new dress or a pocket knife might be an extravagant Christmas gift. Children helped with the chores as soon as they were able to carry a bucket. And if teenagers wanted anything extra, they found a way to make the money they needed. Or they went without.

My generation was directly influenced by our parents and grandparents, our school teachers, the friends we grew up with and the three channels we had available on TV. Today's youth, however, are bombarded with unfiltered messages from many more sources. Every impulse can be chased into a web of self-destruction. Every notion of injustice, every lifestyle variation, every opinion—whether grounded in reality or not—can be supported by someone whose reckless online sharing influences impressionable young minds.

As easily as they can Google how to dye their own hair, they can gain access to every conceivable deviant idea and the people who share them.

Navigating through the mud to realize how amazing life can be is a real challenge for our kids. The path of their lives feels more like quicksand. Taking a step in the wrong direction may seem to be a simple misstep, but the farther they walk in the wrong direction, the deeper and deeper they get pulled into the muck, and the harder it is to pull themselves out.

Certain pressures have affected generations of teens. They need to fit in, to be liked, and have the latest fashion. They feel pressured to make good grades and fight for college admissions and scholarships. Those pressures grow as more kids and their parents become more competitive in every facet of life . . . from travel sports teams, to elaborate theater productions, to winning math and science competitions.

Even more pressure comes from social media.

We have become used to being bombarded with photos and videos of celebrities at every moment of their lives, no matter how private. And every image is critiqued . . . Is their hair perfect? What brand are those jeans? Has she gained weight? Is he dating her?

Because social media sharing is so accessible, every teenager today lives with the pressures of a celebrity. Every look is captured; every word can be analyzed and misinterpreted. Bullies can hide behind computer screens and leave a vulnerable teen feeling fat, skinny, ugly, or unworthy.

If the struggles ended there, I would still be highly concerned about our kids today and would still make it a mission to reach them. But they don't end there.

The pressures on today's youth are magnified with access to vices, and a world filled with more accessible drugs than ever before. Try mixing a cocktail of a 15-year-old-girl who has poor self-esteem with a cell phone camera, unlimited social apps and an unlimited supply of prescription drugs at her disposal. This, unfortunately, happens every day at your local high school.

If you think otherwise, I'm afraid you are living in a bubble of denial. No country, state, community, school, or home is immune to these pressures. Sure, many of our children will make good decisions and resist peer pressure, but please know that they are all being presented with them. You can shelter and protect your kids, but only so much. Christian and private schools are not immune to substance abuse problems. The pressures our kids are under today are real and aren't going away.

So, what do we do? Just stop having kids? Homeschool them and keep them locked away until they are 30? Or do we expose them to everything and hope it will desensitize them to the temptations later?

I will admit that I don't have the perfect answer. Honestly, if anyone sells you on the notion that they do, run the other way!

Through my involvement as a mentor and leader to teens in our church youth group, I feel like I can offer a unique perspective on how we can support our kids through this critical stage of their lives. We have fun together, so they feel comfortable and relaxed around me. They trust me because they know I'm not here to judge them. I am real with them. We have deep discussions about life, religion, and right and wrong.

But please also know that my own sons are just 10 and 12, so I haven't navigated the toughest years as a parent yet.

I know what it's like to be cocky, super confident, a great athlete, popular, a good student, and a leader. I also know what it feels like to be bullied, hated, self-conscious, scared to come to school, different, ashamed, and suicidal. It's amazing how these ranges of emotions were separated from each other by mere months.

As a teenager, I wished I could avoid the negative moments, but God has a funny way of working sometimes. I know He didn't make those bad things happen, but He sure goes to work on those who are broken. He absolutely got me through them. Experiencing those years gave me a new perspective and compassion for those who struggle physically and emotionally. Had I not suffered; I probably would not be able to relate enough to earn the trust of the kids I meet today. To me, earning a kid's trust and offering a safe, open environment to talk and share are vital.

For Youth

For the youth reading this book, I want you to know that no family is perfect, just like no individual is perfect. In the ideal situation, your parents are your biggest fans and would give anything to ensure your happiness and success. Or it may be that your biggest supporter is an extended family member or friend. But even in the best circumstances imaginable, parents and loved ones will sometimes let you down.

So, your parents and your friends' parents aren't perfect (you probably already figured that out). There are some crummy people in this world who will never support us like we need, and that includes some parents. The people we trust to have our backs—no matter what—are sometimes the ones who disappoint us.

I encourage you to understand that we parents are flawed just like you are. The advantage we have is that most of us have experienced some of the challenges you are facing. Hopefully, we have learned from our experience and we can use our wisdom to help you navigate through tough times. Just because we text in complete sentences and still love '80s music doesn't mean that we can't help you get through tough decisions.

For Adults

It's a parent's job to raise good adults, not necessarily to raise good children. Let me repeat. A parent's job is to raise good adults, not necessarily to raise good children.

As adults, we must not be so quick to judge our kids' actions. We must approach our children and teens with concern in our hearts and compassion in our voices.

Houses are not built from the roof down. A solid foundation is the key to a sturdy, well-balanced building. Laying that foundation is what we as parents and mentors should focus on. We don't always get to be the nice guy or girl. We aren't here to be their best friend all the time. It's fun to give our kids everything they want, but it's far more important to give them everything they need. A solid foundation of morals, a sense of security, and unlimited love are all worth so much more than $300 headphones or the latest smartphone. Your dedication to building that foundation will help them navigate the difficulties of the world for the rest of their lives.

Be Present

I always try to convey to parents that their presence is as important as anything. The time you spend with your kids is far more valuable than the money you will spend on them. As adults, they won't remember the $150 shoes or the video game with the best graphics, but they will never forget the quality time you spent with them.

I love wrestling with my kids on the floor. My wife, Des, would love to install hardwoods throughout the first floor, but you can't wrestle on hardwoods! Des can usually get her way with persistence and charm, but believe it or not, I have actually won this battle, so far. My older son is now a middle schooler, but a good rolling around on the floor still brings out a smile from him, and he instantly becomes a little boy again. I love it.

Recently, I somehow tricked my two boys into snuggling with me on the floor in front of the fire as we watched a movie. With one under each arm, I was in heaven. These moments are becoming more and more scarce as they grow older. I was enjoying the warm, fuzzy moment when, without warning, Bodey whacks me and mounts me screaming, "It's WrestleMania time!" Of course, that sparked Tatum's interest. Ninety-nine times out of 100, I'm ready for piledrivers and atomic drops and a loud, obnoxious Ric Flair "Woooooooo!" On this, night, though, I begged them to lay back down and finish the movie because I was tired and just wanted to snuggle. They settled back down, and I could hear B under his breath say, "Ah, man." I felt so terrible.

I thought back to one of my fondest memories of childhood, and I have many. I would be wrestling on the living room floor with my dad. He would toss me around like a dog with a chew toy, but it was so much fun. He was tired after working a full day and then coaching for three hours afterward, but he would tackle and toss and roll and crash until I was worn slam out. And I didn't wear easily. No matter how tired he was, he always found time for me.

So, as I was completely relaxed on the floor with both boys' heads on my chest, and they were resigned to finishing the movie, I surrendered to their desire for horseplay. Subtly, I reached over and found a throw pillow and began whacking the tar out of both of them, yelling "It's WrestleMania time!" It was an all-out brawl after that.

Make time with your kids. It doesn't have to include expensive trips to Disney every year or cruises to the islands. Take a walk in the woods, find a good walking stick and go skip stones in the creek.

Read a book to them every night. Pray with them before bed. Let them tell you what they are thankful for. Do not take this time for granted; you can never get it back. As your kids get older, you will wish you had more time to laugh with them, to build their trust and build that bond.

Even if you invest that time, even if you have a great rapport with your kids, they may not feel comfortable coming to you when they are unsure of something that is going on in their own heart.

Finding another adult whom your kid can go to when there's an issue or a question they may be afraid to ask you as a parent is crucial. Maybe it's a teacher, aunt or uncle, coach, family friend, or youth counselor. Groups like Scouts, 4-H, FFA, Young Life, Boys & Girls Clubs, YMCA, and the Fellowship of Christian Athletes are full of experienced volunteers who have a heart for helping our youth.

It's important our kids have someone that they can trust, but it's equally important that they find the right person, someone with similar values as your family. Find someone who is positive and trying to live their life the right way.

Maybe you can be the person a youth can confide in. Is that a long shot? Do you have the ability to listen? The ability to love? The ability to be trusted? I know you've gone through situations in your life that have given you the experience you can relay to our youth. Are you making yourself available to be that person? You don't have to know all the hottest music or the new lingo to earn a child's trust. Just treat them with respect, and don't judge.

Another word of advice is to be vulnerable. Whether you are serving as a mentor or just building a relationship with a teen, you need to show kids that you are flawed as well. You don't have to tell them EVERYTHING, but being honest and open goes a long way. Let them know that you were once trying to figure out who you were, too.

Step carefully when you tell them you know what it's like to go through what they are going through, or that you understand it. Everyone's situation is different and how they deal with things may be different as well. Acknowledge that you know they are facing a difficult time, and you will do whatever you can to support them and help them get past it.

Children often want to be supported more than they want you to tell them all the answers. They know the right thing to do most of the time.

A friend's teenage daughter started dating a boy from school. At the first dinner with the family, the boy expressed that he didn't care about succeeding in school, and that he had gotten in trouble for saying inappropriate things to a student, whom the father figured to be autistic. The father was obviously unimpressed with the boy, but he didn't demand that his daughter stop seeing him. Instead, the father later asked his daughter what she thought of that situation.

She was conflicted and responded, "I want you to tell me what to do."

"When people see you together, his actions will reflect on you. Just think about how people should treat other people. Can you be a strong enough influence to help him be more respectful?" the dad said. "The decision is yours."

The father spoke with respect and confidence that his daughter would make the right decision.

Empower teens with the courage to make the right decision. Give them the confidence to know that they are never alone, and they can call you anytime. When they do call, they might just need a hug. No words, no advice, just a simple gesture of love and support.

I have always told my youth group kids that there is someone else who is available to talk to them during any tough times . . . God. He doesn't always answer with definitive directives, but I always feel better after we have had a long talk.

Kids need to feel they belong somewhere and are a part of something. They need to feel like their existence matters. Having purpose is powerful. We have limitless opportunities to be difference makers in our worlds. We have to build our youth up and give them the tools to succeed. We want them to understand that they are not a mistake. They were never born to fail. They were intended, by design, to do amazing things.

Don't misconstrue my desire and need to build up our youth and in turn their confidence with babying and giving into their every desire. Some kids have never been told "no," and they struggle as much as those who were deprived in their childhoods.

Loving our youth unconditionally doesn't mean that barriers and rules and structure are avoided. It's the exact opposite. We all have needed structure and rules and expectations to uphold. Creating those environments is healthy as long as the underlying foundation is built on love.

Don't underestimate the influence of your children's peers on their decisions. And remember, your child's sphere of influence includes bad influences in addition to the good. These might include a neighborhood pal who wasn't raised with the values you are instilling in your children. Creating positive structure as a mentor and parent may mean having tough conversations about who your kids associate with. I am nowhere near a preacher but when I talk to our middle school, high school, and college students, I always "preach" to them about how vitally important it is to choose their friends wisely.

Whether I am speaking to one youth or 2,000, I share the same message. *Show me who your friends are, and I will show you what your future looks like.* Let me see who you are spending the majority of your time with, and I will show you how things are panning out for you. I could not be more emphatic about this.

Every adult knows people they grew up with who started hanging around the "wrong crowd." It significantly affected their lives, some permanently. If you follow the wrong crowd and make the same choices, you eventually become the wrong crowd. Then you become the bad influence other parents are warning their kids about.

Getting into the wrong crowd is a slippery slope that is hard to climb out of. Our youth can identify the cliques and groups in their schools that are pushing limits of right and wrong and those that have no regard whatsoever for themselves or others. It's easy to want to fit in and be a part of the crowd.

I was lucky in both high school and college to surround myself with good buddies who had similar life values. We had some great times, and we certainly made our fair share of poor decisions. But our bloopers and regrets were minimized.

I repeatedly tell teens and tweens that they WILL screw up. Inevitably, they will do things that they will look back and say, "What was I thinking?" I encourage them to minimize the "oops," and try not to make those mistakes that will impact them for a lifetime or that could hurt others.

If you are part of the right crowd, you're less likely to make a life-changing mistake. In addition, you can have a positive impact on others. As a youth leader at my church, I encourage my youth to be well rounded, loving and accepting of others. I learned this from my mother, Pam Porter, whose students were often not accepted into traditional middle school social groups. Often, students would snicker behind their backs or avoid them altogether. I've seen the pain, I've felt it, and I would never wish it on someone else.

So, I tell kids to try and be a friend to all. Sure, you can't be BFFs with every person you meet, but you can smile and say a kind word. This becomes a simple habit if you can simply pause your own life long enough to look at the other person and imagine how they feel. Are they uncomfortable making conversation? Are they self-conscious about their skin, their weight, their height? Would a kind word from you make them feel welcome and help them relax and be their true selves?

Let the Voice Guide You

You know the right thing to do if you just listen to the voice.

Yes, I said listen to the voice. I could have avoided so many pitfalls if only I had listened. And there are many times when I did listen to the voice and it saved my rear end.

You know the voice. Just as you are about to make a tough choice or take questionable action, the voice in your head asks, "Is this a good idea?" Almost EVERY poor choice I have made in my life, I heard that voice. And I ignored it.

Whose voice is this? Is it God? Is it your mom? Is it the Holy Spirit's voice? I could agree with all of those. If you know this voice I speak of, consider yourself blessed. Sometimes, it sounds like the voice is just telling you to not have any fun. But you should consider yourself extremely lucky to have this sometimes-annoying voice in your head. Every person you have ever known—even your sweet granny—has made many terrible choices. But she will probably tell you that she made bad choices because she didn't listen to the voice.

The fact that you hear this voice is proof that you know right from wrong.

There are many who never hear it, and they are doomed to make mistakes when they are confronted by a negative influence. I pray for them because they do not have a positive guiding force in their life.

You, however, have a set of values that help you know deep down the correct thing to do. Sometimes, you may think the voice is inhibiting your freedom. You may choose to ignore the voice and face no negative consequences. But that's a gamble. Just ask yourself this—When you last disappointed your parents or your spouse or felt ashamed for your own actions, did the voice speak to you prior to the mistake? More than likely it did.

Life is full of choices. Millions of choices. God was extremely generous to allow us to make our own choices. These choices help define who we are—the good, the bad, and all the gray areas that make us all unique human beings.

You should listen to that voice because years and years of knowledge have fueled that voice. That voice knows most things. I beg you to listen to it. I pray every day that I will listen to that voice. I pray every day to be better than yesterday.

As you make sound decisions, that voice becomes more powerful and you learn to trust it. Your future, your reputation, your integrity is defined by whether you listen to or ignore the voice.

Chapter 14: Inspired by Zig

Words of Wisdom

I knew I was called to speak. But as I tried to figure out whether motivational speaking was a realistic career choice for me, I had two issues that kept me from diving in headfirst. 1.) I had a family to support, and the economic uncertainty of a speaking career would certainly create some stress. 2.) I had an internal ethical debate. If God had chosen me to share my message, was it okay for me to profit from it?

So, I sought the advice of some of the most successful, noble people in the world of motivational speaking. I had the privilege and honor to become connected with the family of the late Zig Ziglar. Zig spent most of his life motivating the masses. In his lifetime, he reached more than 250 million people across the globe. He was the author of more than a dozen books and was an innovator in what he calls Automobile University—audio tools to listen to in the car. He changed thousands of lives with a message of positivity, and he shaped some of the most successful people in the world.

I have never met a single person who has a cross word to say about Zig. He had an unmatched passion for improving people's lives in areas he described as the Wheel of Life: Mental, Spiritual, Physical, Family, Financial, Personal, and Career. I had the opportunity to spend a week at Ziglar Headquarters and study under Zig's son, Tom Ziglar, and his team. I soaked up a wealth of knowledge that I could seamlessly integrate into the material and story that I had been presenting. What a powerful combination! One powerful story and the golden nuggets of how to implement immediate change in all the core areas in your life.

I was first turned onto Zig's legend when I was selling real estate. He helped define real sales to me, and I am forever grateful that he was able to help me. Of course, Zig had no idea that a young father in Wilmington, North Carolina, was heeding his advice and using it to improve his practice.

Years later, I sat in Ziglar headquarters, waiting to speak to his son and daughters. I was going to be groomed to continue his legacy by sharing what he spent 40 years creating. What an honor! Tom deserves a huge amount of credit for opening my eyes about an issue I had struggled with for many years . . . accepting money for something I am just supposed to do.

Should I be getting paid to serve God's calling on my life? I felt like I wasn't supposed to prosper for helping people. I was so thankful to be able to inspire and help other people, and I felt I should do it solely to help others, just like others had helped me. And that's exactly what I had done the previous 20 years!

Tom and I sat in his office and I shared with him how torn I was to receive compensation. His advice was very comforting. "Do you have something that people need? Do you provide a service that helps to change lives?" he asked. I answered with confidence, "Yes!" "Then you have an obligation to sell that to people. You have an obligation to give that service to as many people as possible. If you don't receive compensation for speaking, you aren't going to help very many people."

He was right. I would be forced to continue working a 40+ hour job to take care of my family's financial needs and on occasion find some time to speak to a local group. I knew I had to get over my hesitation. Millions of people spend their hard-earned money to try and improve their lives. Many times, these methods are unproductive, and sometimes, they are downright deceptive.

I had testimonials from people who said my presentation made a huge difference in their lives. Tom helped me understand that the next person who needed my message might be working at a factory in South Dakota, and if I was still working a day job in Wilmington, NC, that person might never hear my message. I have an obligation to share my message with as many people as possible, he said. After talking to Tom, I felt like I had permission to move forward.

Not long after my week of training with the Ziglars, I was selected to be part of the former Zig Ziglar International Team, where my opportunities to touch more and more people would be realized. One of my favorite things about having an association with the Ziglar family is that I never have to compromise my faith and beliefs because Zig never hid his, even after being advised by many that he should never mix his faith and his speaking.

I understand when to share the religious side of the story and when not to, depending on the audience and situation. Like Zig, I understand that sometimes the message needs to be more motivational and less spiritual. When I speak to companies and conferences in the secular world, I spend less time talking about God and Christianity. But those who believe still hear it in my presentations, and those who don't might be intrigued enough to ask questions. If anyone asks how I was able to overcome so much, I don't hesitate to tell them the full story.

With Tom's encouragement and support, I took a leap of faith and closed my financial practice. I vowed to concentrate on being the best speaker I could possibly be and see how many people I could reach.

Some of my closest friends expressed their concern about my decision. Some, even those who had been in a room full of adults mesmerized by my story, felt like it was a gamble for me to become a full-time speaker and still provide financial security for my family. I had doubts, too. In my mind, "motivational" and "keynote" speakers were traditionally immensely successful business people who were former CEOs of Fortune 500 companies. I had not built a business empire or supervised hundreds of employees. I'd had success with my business endeavors, but not to that extent.

That philosophy was quickly debunked. Just because you are successful in one world doesn't automatically qualify you to be successful in the other. It takes a special kind of person to get in front of 2,000 people and entertain them for two hours, while engraving a lasting impression on their lives to the point where they are motivated to make changes.

I am forever thankful for all that I have gone through in my life—the good and the bad—and I am equally blessed to have the opportunity to enter the lives of everyone sitting in the audience. If they are seeking some positivity or clarity, the message can truly inspire them. You don't need a business pedigree or a sultan's wealth to reach a person's heart.

I have listened to hundreds of professional speakers, studying their techniques, vocal styles and audience engagement. You might even call me a speaker snob because it takes a really powerful speaker to keep me engaged.

With all of my studies, I have found a consistent tactic of the most effective speakers—they deliver a message of optimism grounded in truth. I refuse to be the generic keynote speaker who will stare into your eyes and tell you that you can be anything you want to be. Unfortunately, that's just not true! I wish it was, and I am sorry if I have crushed your bubble.

I really wanted to play in the NFL, but that's never going to happen no matter how hard I try. I do, however, believe that we can accomplish things that seem to be longshots, and I believe we are far more capable of being more than we give ourselves credit for. If you are stuck in an unfulfilling world or an unrewarding job that simply pays the bills, I encourage you to not settle. Seek something that is a passion.

Please don't misunderstand what I am trying to tell you . . . I'm not telling you to walk into the office tomorrow morning, tell your boss to kiss your rump and strut out the door. As my Dad always reminded me, your responsibility is to provide for your family. I didn't quit everything and chase after my dream. I made sure that my calling and what I wanted to do for the remainder of my life would support those I care about.

I do not take for granted that I have been called by God to serve his purpose. I have learned that God can turn horrible circumstances into amazing things when you trust him and pray for His help. Decades after my amputation, I get to travel across the country, meeting new people every week. And I get to inspire them to reach their potential, professionally and spiritually. I have the greatest career in the entire world!

The people and companies that I have had the privilege to speak to fuel me with their passion to be better. Everyone wants to be better. They may suppress it or avoid it for many reasons. Many don't think they are deserving. Some don't realize the potential that lies within them. Some have been convinced that this is as good as they will ever be. Others simply aren't motivated enough or focused enough to put in the effort it will take to improve themselves.

Some people don't even realize that improvement is possible. Those are the toughest ones to crack. I have yet to meet someone who is truly perfect, although I have met dozens who think they are. But they aren't the majority. Most crave to be better people. I pray every day that God will help me be the person that I truly aspire to be. I realize I will never get there, but as long as I am getting closer every day, I am satisfied.

Your Three Lives

I have found three main areas of life that challenge all of us. Personal Life, Work Life, and Community Life. My goal is to help people improve in those three areas, and they are impossible to separate from one another.

If you aren't happy in your personal life or if things aren't going well at home, it can directly affect your work. If work is going poorly and you bring that negative energy home with you, it can cause friction with your spouse or your children, who might feel like they are causing your anger or stress. If you are struggling with your work life or family life, I guarantee that it will have a negative impact on your ability to be a productive member of your community. You are so wrapped up with YOU that you won't even notice those who really need your help. Being involved in your community is vital to both you and others. One of my favorite Zig quotes is "You can have everything in life you want, if you'll just help enough other people get what they want."

I'm not trying to tell you that I can fix all of these areas for you in my hour and a half keynote or full-day interactive presentations, but my hope is that I can light a fire inside you to realize your worth, inspire your potential, and help give you nuggets that you can refer to as you start to make changes.

I am so blessed that I have experienced such a rollercoaster life, including my professional careers. I feel like I can relate to many people in various stages of their lives. I am not suggesting I am a guru who knows it all; quite the opposite. But I have learned that certain characteristics improve your ability to motivate people enough to make change and inspire them to believe that they are worthy of such change.

Some of those characteristics are: You have to be willing to listen and you have to be able to love. You have to be genuine. You have to convey your message in a way that will be entertaining enough to keep an audience's attention. It must come from your heart. I spoke for 20 years before I ever took a paycheck. I LOVE to make a crowd laugh until their stomachs hurt, cry because they are moved by the story, and be so captivated that they are on the edge of their seat the entire ride. It's so much fun.

Chapter 15:
Full Circle

Carl's Journey

After rejuvenating my speaking career, I was inspired to write a book. I wanted to have the opportunity to inspire those who may never have a chance to hear my presentation. I hoped those who were inspired at a presentation would share the book with someone in their lives who might need a message of hope, resilience and purpose.

As I wrote this book, I realized I couldn't do it justice without mentioning Carl Sherman.

You see, I wasn't the only person permanently injured that tragic Sunday afternoon at Tucker Lake . . .

Carl Sherman suffered more injuries that day than anyone else. His scars were deeper and more painful. Like me, his life was forever changed.

Carl had been driving the boat.

Every pain I felt on the outside, Carl felt on the inside. For every scar that is visible on my battered leg, there is a deeper, grislier scar on Carl's heart. For every second I suffered through physical pain, Carl suffered emotionally for hours.

Before the accident, Carl was simply a devoted father volunteering his time to help give a bunch of kids a childhood they would never forget.

At Tucker Lake, though, something had gone horribly wrong. As the adult in charge, Carl was wracked with guilt. After I had been hit and the boat was turned off, several adults helped Carl out of the boat and walked him away from the scene. Distraught and inconsolable, he couldn't have handled seeing the carnage.

Over the next few days, the uncertainty of my survival was eating him alive. Even after it became clear that I would likely survive the accident, Carl wondered if I would ever walk again, if I would ever get married and have children. Would I live the rest of my life in a wheelchair? How would my parents react to him?

While I was receiving all the newspaper headlines and "Get Well" cards, Carl sought asylum in his own home. I had professional athletes and political figures stopping by my hospital room and sending warm wishes, but Carl isolated himself on an island of grief with only his immediate family to support him.

After about a week, one of the dads of the Ski Heels crew called Carl and told him they were on the way to pick him up and take him to the hospital to see me. Carl's anxiety and fear were at an all-time high, but he also knew this had to happen.

Once he arrived, the long hallways of Duke University Medical Center were all that stood between him and this 15-year-old kid whose life he felt responsible for changing forever. The waves of emotion were paralyzing.

As he turned the corner on the fifth-floor pediatric wing, his gaze met my parents, who were talking with friends in the waiting room. Without hesitation, both of my parents stood and embraced Carl with the tightest and most loving hugs. His body melted into their arms.

My parents had never for a minute doubted the goodness in Carl Sherman's heart. They knew Carl was struggling with guilt, they felt his pain, and they showered him with love and support.

Carl dried his tears, got an update on my present condition, and braced himself for the next encounter. My mother escorted him to my room. She re-introduced us, and then she turned right around and left the two of us in the room alone, closing the door behind her.

I was medicated and fighting for my life, so I don't remember seeing Carl or anything that was said between us.

After a little time passed, Carl exited the room and returned to the waiting room where everyone was anxiously waiting to hear how it went. As he described our conversation to friends, my mom came back into my room to see how I was doing. After only a minute or two with me, she rejoined the group.

"Chad's in his room crying," she told Carl, tears streaming down her face. "But he's not crying for himself. He's worried about you. He said he feels so sorry for what you are going through. He needs you to be okay."

Those words left a lasting impression on a lot of people that day. It was one of those moments when God graciously allowed me to show a heart of compassion. I thank my incredible parents, who raised their children to be compassionate and empathetic toward others. God was in that room that day for sure.

Life continued to be a challenge for Carl throughout the next few years, as the Tucker Lake incident played on a continuous loop in his brain. He wondered what he could have done differently. He hoped that I was doing okay. Rarely a day went by when his stomach didn't experience those uncomfortable butterflies of anxiety.

For years, Carl fought depression. His relationships with his wife and children were compromised. He woke up night after night in a cold sweat from the nightmares.

He sought out a therapist and learned to cope with the grief that gripped him. He took solace in my accomplishments, but sometimes a trigger would cause him to relive the whole experience.

Years after the accident, Carl took up drag racing as a hobby to replace the boat he no longer drove. On one of many trips across North Carolina to a drag strip on the outskirts of a small town with more barbecue joints than pizza shops, Carl passed Tucker Lake.

"Did you hear the story about the kid who got run over by a boat at this lake?" his friend asked, not knowing Carl was even there that day. "It was a really gruesome sight—he lost one leg and nearly lost the other!"

"Is that right?" Carl said, hoping his disinterest would thwart the conversation. Usually, he could find something else to talk about. But that didn't stop the daggers from ripping into his heart and his mind.

Reconnecting

About four years after my accident, I received a phone call from Carl. I imagine the receiver felt like a cinder block in his hand. But his desire to help another soul gave him the strength to overcome whatever anxiety he had. Carl reached out to me because he had read a story in the newspaper, and he thought some young men needed our help.

When Carl called me, he had no reason to worry. Nobody in my family ever blamed Carl for what happened. We understood it was a total accident that could have happened to anyone. My parents made phone calls and sent letters to Carl to express their feelings. And on those rare occasions when they got to see him, they always wrapped him in tight hugs.

I was so happy to hear from him. I had recovered better than doctors ever imagined, and my life was full. I was busy with college life, sports, girls, partying and studying. I wasn't constantly reliving that horrible day like Carl had been. I'm sure my enthusiasm to reconnect with him was comforting.

The article Carl called me about told the details of a young driver on his way home from a baseball game. He had seen an interstate exit sign too late, tried to make a last-second turn and flipped his vehicle. When he flipped the car, one of his friends lost a leg; another lost his life. The accident rocked a small community and left lives forever changed.

As he read me the article, I could hear something in Carl's voice that clearly spoke to me. This was our moment. This was the moment that two men, who will forever be linked by a tragic circumstance, could write a new chapter for the benefit of helping others.

Few people know the burden of guilt that comes with feeling like you are responsible for such a tragedy. But Carl does.

And few people understand the hope and faith it requires to survive a life-altering catastrophe. But I do.

When Carl called, I readily agreed to meet with him and go see those baseball players.

I remember sitting in the living room with the young amputee. His parents sat in the corner holding each other's hands hoping that our visit would help in some way. Carl sat quietly behind me listening to me tell the story that he knew all too well, but had never heard from my point of view.

There were waves of emotion from everyone in the room. Tears. Laughter. Hope. Encouragement.

For Carl, watching me use my tragedy to help heal someone was a dose of medicine that would help propel him to healing himself.

However, the true healing began with the next stop.

Carl got a chance to share his story to that young driver—the boy who had unintentionally killed his friend. Carl felt a sense of purpose that had been lacking for so long. He began to see how his life could be used to benefit someone else's, how his suffering could be used to help lessen another's grief.

We may never know the level of impact that Carl had on that grief-stricken young man that day, but I know for a fact that the time spent was healing for the family and it helped that boy. He will never forget that visit, and he knows that he is not alone in this world and he is loved. Carl made sure of that. The embrace between two strangers as they parted ways was exactly what they both needed.

Like me, Carl had his "Why me?" moments. And when he met that young man and saw with his own eyes that I truly was going to be okay, he reclaimed some of his former self. Nobody saw it more clearly than his wife. In her eyes, that was the day she started to get her husband back.

Carl continued to patch up his life and relationships and move on to becoming the person he wanted to be. I was just starting my journey as a young man, and so I didn't have a hint as to how many people might be inspired by our story.

Carl and I drifted apart again, and we didn't speak for years. This wasn't due to any animosity, but rather just life circumstances.

So, as I was writing this book, I reached out to Carl. I needed his perspective on the day that changed my life forever. Just as he once needed to know I was okay, I needed to know that he was okay.

I met him for lunch, and we talked freely about what we both had gone through.

It was a great day. We laughed. We cried. We told stories that neither of us had heard before. Carl told me specifics that I did not know about how the accident happened. Nothing was left on the table.

We both acknowledged that day that we both have a responsibility, a responsibility to use our lives for the betterment of others.

Our relationship could have gone in so many directions after that summer day in 1991. There could have been anger, resentment, hatred. But because the Porters and the Shermans chose forgiveness, compassion, and love, our story has a happy ending.

We all have relationships that have gone in the wrong direction. We have been hurt by someone, and we have caused our share of pain. The anger you harbor toward someone else will ultimately only hurt you. Life is too short to spend it full of bitterness and hate.

If Carl and I, after all the pain we have experienced, can come together in love and transform that into a mission to help others, maybe we can inspire you to reach out and repair your broken relationships too.

I know that you are strong enough and brave enough. Let go of that pain. Forgive. Love. Accept. Then take that positive energy and spread it to others who need it as well.

There will be a day soon where I will have Carl join me on stage to move, inspire, and change lives. It will be an amazing day.

Chapter 16:
It's Time to
Make a Difference

I am so blessed. Far beyond what I deserve.

I am excited about what is in store for you and me. I am excited to continue my mission of trying to inspire and motivate as many people as I can across the world. I want to reach those who have lost hope, who need to feel loved and supported, or who need a word of encouragement. I want to stir the hearts of those who need direction in their professional and personal lives and help them reach new levels of growth.

How about you? What are your plans? Have they changed? Who will you serve? Who will you inspire? How will you reach out to others and make a difference?

I hope those questions excite you. I hope that you are eager to discover your story.

Many people need an emotional or spiritual lift. By discovering your gifts and your story, you open up the opportunities to be the light for those in need. When your heart is in it, you can make a difference.

Our lives are not simply about ourselves. Our lives are enriched by what we do for others. Our legacy is about who we have served and where we have made a positive impact.

What sparks your heart? Where do you feel like there is a need that you can get behind with passion and selflessness? Who can you help? What talents do you have that can be utilized for the betterment of your community? Who needs you to advocate for them? I know for a fact someone needs you and craves to hear your story.

We will all leave a legacy.

You will be remembered for either building people up or tearing people down. I have no doubt that if you are finishing this book that you would rather be remembered for all the good you brought to this world.

I recently attended a funeral for a good friend's father. As I listened to the stories about him, the memories of his character and his good deeds, I wondered what would be said at my funeral. Who would show up? Would it be standing room only? Who would stand up to tell a story and what would they say? How would I be remembered?

Have you ever asked yourself these questions?

I want to be remembered for only good things that I've done. It's not in my DNA to want to hurt anyone. Does that mean that I have never hurt someone? Absolutely not, but it doesn't stop me from praying and trying every day to be better and better.

I can't change the past. I can apologize and ask for forgiveness. On some occasions, an apology will help right the wrongs that have occurred. Unfortunately, there are other occasions when it won't, and those are the moments that are the hardest to bear.

I want to leave a good impression on everyone I meet. I'm sure you do too. I have learned over the years, that no matter how hard I try, it's an unreasonable expectation. Even with serious introspection, it's not easy to accept that you can't please everybody. But you'll never be able to move forward if you punish yourself for how someone else perceives you.

What do you want to be remembered for? What words would you like to be used to describe you when your time on earth is over? Make a list of those words. Are you pleased with where you are on your path? What do you find praiseworthy in others that you might also want to apply to yourself?

You have a story and a message to share. I hope you use it to encourage those who are struggling to find their path to reach their purpose.

If you aren't where you need to be, you are not alone, my friend. But you can take comfort that you are among a vast group of people who have honorable intentions and hope to continue to better themselves. I have no doubt that the words that you want to be remembered for are absolutely attainable. When your desire to be a better person fuels sustained effort and dedication, you can get to where you need to be.

Many people have expressed to me that they have the hardest time forgiving themselves for past mistakes. It's so hard to do. It means you have a heart and you care. You feel bad about your mistakes. That's a good human quality. But it's a quality you don't have to learn to cope with.

Why? You have already been forgiven! How cool is that? God made the ultimate sacrifice for you by putting his Son on the cross to die for your sins. You are forgiven by Him. So, if the most powerful Being ever can forgive you, then you can learn to forgive yourself.

I say that as if I never have those same feelings. I have trouble letting go of past mistakes too. I know that I am forgiven by the One who matters the most, but in order for me to ultimately be the person I want to become, I have to forgive myself.

They key is to learn from your mistakes. You must grow from your failures. You will never lose with that attitude. Ever! You win, or you grow. Some of the most valuable life lessons and moments of growth come from your mistakes.

The time is now.

Now is your time to start becoming the person that you want to become. Now is the time for you to start living the life that you were created to live. No matter what you are waiting for, or what excuses you've used to put it off, now is your moment to start your journey.

Your first step in this journey is fixing whatever worries, issues, mistakes, or situations that are holding you back. You won't be able to give yourself sufficiently to others until you have invested enough time in getting to a good place in your personal life.

Wouldn't you love to know that one day you reached your pinnacle? How rewarding would it be to know that you achieved your highest possible potential during your lifetime?

Well, I hate to break it to you, but most people will never get there. You may never experience your fullest potential. Before you slam the book closed, let me explain why and offer a solution.

Your potential and personal growth builds upon itself as your life goes forward. Getting stuck in a rut and going through the motions keeps you from realizing your potential. Are you currently just doing "enough?" Are your goals to be a good enough parent, a decent spouse, an okay employee and business owner, or to be someone who every once in a while, does something positive in your community? Maybe you do just enough to pat yourself on the back, but you know you could do so much more.

I hope that you have larger aspirations. If you want to be the best you possible, you have to give the most important things in your life every drop of effort you can muster. No longer are you allowed to just go through the motions, doing just enough at home, work and in your community. You owe it to yourself and those around you to give 100 percent to those things you deem important. If you are in it, be in it!

In order to be successful, you can't do everything. You can't be everything for everybody. That can be hard to swallow. You must choose what is truly important to you and make those things your priorities. It may also mean that you cut some negative things out of your life. Those things might be toxic people, bad habits, or worthless activities. You know what's right for you.

You are worth it. You deserve it. Don't shortchange your life because you didn't give the effort. The fight is worth it. Giving up is easy. You owe it to yourself and those who love you to fight!

The best thing about these moments are that you get to choose your attitude and your path. Find your support. Get a trustworthy accountability partner who will hold you to your goals. Someone who will encourage you when times get tough and give you that hug when you need it the most. Feed yourself with positivity.

Zig Ziglar said it best:

"You are who you are, and you are where you are by what has gone into your mind. You change what you are and where you are by changing what goes into your mind."

Wouldn't you agree that everything you are today and who you have become is a result of what has gone into your brain? You are a product of all your life experiences, everything you've been taught, read, or heard. If you agree with this, and this has made you into the person you are, then you will agree that if you want to change something about yourself you need to change the input, the things you allow into your head.

If you want something different, you have to DO something different. For every person, that will look extremely different, but the concept works. Change your ways. Find friends who have a more positive outlook. Read more positive material, watch something encouraging, listen to something that motivates you in the right way. Motivation is like bathing—it doesn't last. So, you need to do it daily.

My Four H's:

I often challenge my audiences to recognize their impact. Your impact will ultimately define you in the eyes of others. Your impact will help shape your legacy. I think that we can become so entrenched in our own shortcomings that we don't realize our impact on those around us—good and bad.

I challenge you to embrace your impact. Use it for good. It's amazing how the small things you do in life make such a huge difference. Here are my four H's that are simple and may work for you. They don't take much effort and can go a long way to help someone who's having a tough day.

Practice these simple rules and see what kind of impact you have on others. You might even be surprised by how you feel about yourself. Practice the 4 H's: Hi, Handshake, Held door, and a Hug.

1. Hi: This simple acknowledgement can brighten a person's day, or spark a conversation. In the South, it's customary to greet someone you pass on the street, share an elevator with or make eye contact with on the bus.

2. Handshake: This sign of respect can convey warmth and confidence and offer reassurance of your good intentions. A firm handshake can go a long way.

3. Held Door: This shows others that you are not just thinking about yourself, but you notice them as well. It lets someone know that they are important enough to wait on. When you see a child holding the door for someone, you know his parents raised him right.

4. Hug: Sometimes, you don't have the right words to make everything better. We need to get outside of our comfort zones sometimes and embrace someone with a good ol embrace. If you have ever met me, you know . . . I'm a hugger.

Those aren't hard. But they are quite powerful and are contagious. Impactful.

Selfless giving is the key. If you struggle finding happiness in your life, go make someone else happy and see if that helps!

Do you need permission to start? No. But just in case you do, here you go.

I give you permission to let go of all that has been holding you back. I give you permission to hold your head high no matter what wrong you have done. I give you permission to look in your mirror and start to love again that person looking back at you. I give you permission to start becoming who you've always dreamed you wanted to be.

- ☐ You are worthy.
- ☐ You deserve happiness.
- ☐ You are capable of amazing things.
- ☐ You are supported.
- ☐ You were made in a perfect image.
- ☐ You are not alone.
- ☐ You are loved!

Final word

If that boat had never run over my leg, I might have become a pro football player. I might have made millions of dollars, bought a 200-foot yacht and lived in an 8,000 square foot mansion. I hope I would have been the Jim Ritcher of my generation, visiting a sick kid in the hospital and then coming back another day because the kid was asleep. But I'll never know.

I do know it's unlikely that I would have met people as important to me as the kids I coach in Miracle League baseball games. I wouldn't have had the opportunity to invest my time in guiding the youth group at Pine Valley United Methodist Church. I would have never understood the obstacles the Port City Spokesmen overcome every day just to drive to a basketball practice, get out of their cars and get into the gym.

Most importantly, I would never have had a chance to share my story with thousands of kids and adults across the United States. I wouldn't have made the connection with a 45-year-old woman, who, prompted by my speech, texted her mother "I love you." That text initiated the first conversation between them in 25 years. Her tears of joy and appreciation will never be forgotten. They keep my fire lit to continue reaching as many people as I can.

If I hadn't been in that accident, I might never have met my wonderful wife and I wouldn't be raising the two precious souls that are my sons.

I would never wish my tragic accident on another person. But that fateful day is largely responsible for who I am today.

I get to travel the world. I get to meet people every week. Some share amazing stories; others just need a sliver of hope to hang onto. And when I return home to my family, I know I've made a difference in people's lives.

Sometimes, with my youth group, I'll share stories of my travels and the people I've met.

Upon hearing about the places I get to visit, and the people I get to inspire, a girl in my youth group left me speechless.

"You know, Mr. Chad," she said. "Losing your leg is the best thing that ever happened to you."

She's right.

Chad's Acknowledgements

It's been over 7 years of consideration and over 2 ½ years writing, but I am so excited that *Severed Dreams, Reconstructing Your Purpose* is here! I am thrilled that you have chosen to spend your valuable time learning my story and hopefully drawing inspiration along the way.

I literally pinch myself sometimes because I am so blessed to be able to live this life doing what I love and helping others along the way. I am so lucky and thankful to have gone through the trials of my life as they have shaped me into the man I am today. But none of this was possible without the support of all those who have played rolls in this journey.

I need to start with the loves of my life . . . Desiree, Tatum, and Bodey. Without you, I would be empty. Thank you for always being there for me and understanding that, although Dad is on the road quite a bit, you are always on my mind and number one in my heart. Everything I do is for you. I want to also thank my sister, Elise, for always being a best friend and loving my boys as her own.

I want to thank Mike for being patient, encouraging, and professional. I have told you many times during this journey that if it wasn't for you, this wouldn't have happened. You helped a guy, who barely reads books, write one!

There is no one who deserves more thanks than my absolutely amazing parents. They have always been there for me with unwavering support. They stand for all that is right. They are great examples of what parents should be. Happy 50th wedding Anniversary, Mom and Dad! I dedicate this book to you. I hope I have made you proud!

About the Co-Author

Mike Voorheis grew up digging potatoes and skipping rocks in Lucasville, Ohio. He attended the University of Rio Grande, where he was more ballplayer than athlete. He dabbled for decades in newspapers, where he was more writer than journalist. He now lives in Wilmington, NC, where he is more local than Yankee.

He would like to thank Frank, Tania, Zachary and Jenna for the inspiration and encouragement to keep writing. Thanks also to Chad, for letting me help tell his story, and for the patience and perseverance to complete it.

Mike dedicates his work on this book to his father, Roger, and late mother, Donna Jean, whose devotion to her children was an example to us all.

For more information, videos and booking information for Chad, please visit his website.

ChadPorter.org

Made in the USA
Monee, IL
18 April 2021

65070955R00105